I0030397

PREPARING EMPLOYEES FOR RETIREMENT

Leon Steyn

TALENT MANAGEMENT SERIES

Copyright © KR Publishing and Leon Steyn

All reasonable steps have been taken to ensure that the contents of this book do not, directly or indirectly, infringe any existing copyright of any third person and, further, that all quotations or extracts taken from any other publication or work have been appropriately acknowledged and referenced. The publisher, editors and printers take no responsibility for any copyright infringement committed by an author of this work.

Copyright subsists in this work. No part of this work may be reproduced in any form or by any means without the written consent of the publisher or the author.

While the publisher, editors and printers have taken all reasonable steps to ensure the accuracy of the contents of this work, they take no responsibility for any loss or damage suffered by any person as a result of that person relying on the information contained in this work.

All cases are for illustrative purposes only and the intent is not to evaluate the performance of an organisation.

First published in 2018.

ISBN: 978-1-86922-820-0
eISBN: 978-1-86922-821-7 (ePDF)

Published by KR Publishing
P O Box 3954
Randburg
2125
Republic of South Africa

Tel: (011) 706-6009
Fax: (011) 706-1127
E-mail: orders@knowres.co.za
Website: www.kr.co.za

Typesetting, layout and design: Cia Joubert, cia@knowres.co.za
Cover design: Marlene de'Lorme, marlene@knowres.co.za
Editing and proofreading: Valda Strauss, valda@global.co.za
Project management: Cia Joubert, cia@knowres.co.za

Table of Contents

About the author

Leon *Ernest* Steyn is an entrepreneur, master facilitator-trainer in the Frankfurt Am Main Area, Germany. He's worked nationally and internationally for over 31 years in the fields of general management, organisational development, coaching, consulting and skills development. Using his international experience, he blends global trends with local conditions. He's moderated a wide spectrum of seminars and workshops during the last 20 years, is the author of the book *Transformation in 28 Days* and has co-developed and produced a video series for the Services SETA. He currently holds a MPhil from the University of Cape Town, as well as numerous local and international qualifications in the fields of coaching, NLP and leadership. Leon is passionate about helping people to find their 'AHA!' moment and then guiding them to the next level!

Introduction

"When I was a boy of 14, my father was so ignorant I could hardly stand to have the old man around. But when I got to be 21, I was astonished at how much the old man had learned in seven years."
— Mark Twain

Although written many years ago, when there were less people on the planet, and most definitely before the various industrial revolutions had rewritten the history books, this quotation by Mark Twain clearly proves that experience is a most precious thing to have. We know that. We, HR people, know that. We, HR people, know that and sometimes do not use that wisdom to attract, nurture and care for the very vessels of experience – the people. By reading this book, you will be reminded of the importance of "Pushing the people, while you hug them" to quote Brand Pretorius, former leader of the McCarthy Motor Group. The pragmatic approach and useful checklists should contribute to an employee retirement plan (ERP) which is easy to use and to explain to the people managing the process. You can rest assured that the guidelines, suggestions and experiences are from real life and that the stress related to employees facing the uncertainty of retirement, is not to be underestimated – it is a very big event in any person's (including my own) life. The following story explains this happening...

The employee across the table from me was angry, really angry and it took me by surprise! The accusation caught me totally unawares, "So, am I no longer good enough?!"

Then it dawned on me... our planned chat about their retirement had triggered a flood of emotions that I was clearly not prepared for. The discussion ended well, albeit with some serious preoccupation on my part as to why this employee responded in this "negative" manner – after all, we all *know* that sooner or later we will be retiring. The reality only hits home, it seems, when an employee is actually faced with the actual event now being entered in a calendar.

This experience during my tenure as Divisional Executive: Training and Development and later on as Human Resources Director of another large company, was the catalyst for the development and use of a most rewarding and valuable programme – Preparing Employees for Retirement.

- ■ Will it not be a happy day for recruiters when they can fill all their vacancies with competent people?
- ■ Will it not be a happy day for retirees when they can be offered the opportunity to add value, after their retirement date!
- ■ And would it not be a happy day, also, for a Chief Human Resources Officer (CHRO) or CEO to build a bridge between these two groups of people and retain competent people?

Leaders will know that, "poaching" is merely a euphemism for explaining that the current employer did not adequately value the employee and that the employee resigned! During Peter's – an operations manager of the company I worked at – exit interview he was most surprised to learn that he had been nominated by his manager as a successor to a retiree; his manager had never bothered to tell Peter that he was valued, that his excellent performance had been noticed and that he was officially on the company succession plan! In this book you will learn, and be reminded with examples, that communication trumps intent every time.

Now is the best time to get started with our easy-to-use, practical and most rewarding ERP. And the opportunity to leave a legacy for a long, long time. After all, people remember *how* you make them feel long after they have forgotten *what* you did for them.

Mature and prudent companies have long realised that prospective retirees are a grand source of wisdom, skill and stability and these companies have decent employee retirement plans firmly established. If you do not yet live this maturity and prudence or you would like to revamp your employee retirement strategy, then this book is for you.

Amongst others, you will find the following valuable tips to easily prepare your employee retirement plan by:

- **Preparing** the employer and retiree for a great new experience.
- **Communicating** the new experience with all stakeholders, timeously and comprehensively.
- **Ensuring** that fairness and transparency prevails.
- **Supporting** and guiding the retiree.
- **Offering** further training for the retiree to help clarify the "how".
- **Celebrating** the start of the new journey with a party!

Preparing Employees for Retirement is a must for any leader who is serious about talent retention. This authoritative guide gives great practical advice in the form of tips, summaries and checklists to help any human resources person plan, implement and execute a successful employee retirement plan.

Who is this book for?

This book is intended for the CEO, Chief Human Resources Officer, HR Manager or Line Manager who is serious about retaining, developing and retraining top talent with the knowledge, skills and great attitude, to help create a sustainable enterprise. The intention is to provide broad guidelines, with some relevant detailed toolkits, on a best-practice level, on how to retain good people post their usual (or prescribed) retirement date.

Although the type of process and the extent of preparing employees for retirement may be different, organisations both large and small should have some form of labour force plan, which incorporates the retirement phase. This book is not intended to be an exhaustive resource for retirement plans, but is aimed at providing sound, tried-and-tested concepts and processes for the mindful and 4.0 thinking executive and manager, to easily implement with confidence. I have also included references for some literature and a few websites that provide more depth to some of the concepts I cover.

I have made use of the two genders interchangeably in the book to prevent any perception of gender bias. In addition, I have included a generic retirement process that you can adapt and customise based on your needs.

How to use this book

First of all, be prepared to make and accept some changes – small or big changes require resilience, commitment and an adaptive spirit. The benefits of designing and implementing a best practice Employee Retirement Procedure (ERP) far outweigh the efforts, short-term disruption and some discomfort. The age-old saying, "No pain, no gain" applies to these circumstances too.

Although it is hoped that the information provided in this guide is easy to use and simple to apply, reality and logic should prevail at all times. Do not rush into the new ERP and potentially cause more harm than good through well-intended, but misguided efforts. Take your time, work through this guide meticulously so that you and your company can reap the rewards of dealing with retiring employees (who most probably served the organisation very well, for many years) in the most humane and productive manner possible.

For ease of reference, a flow chart is provided on the following pages to help you plan and track your progression and to assist you in bringing it all together most efficiently and in a well-structured manner.

Flow Chart of Preparing Employees for Retirement

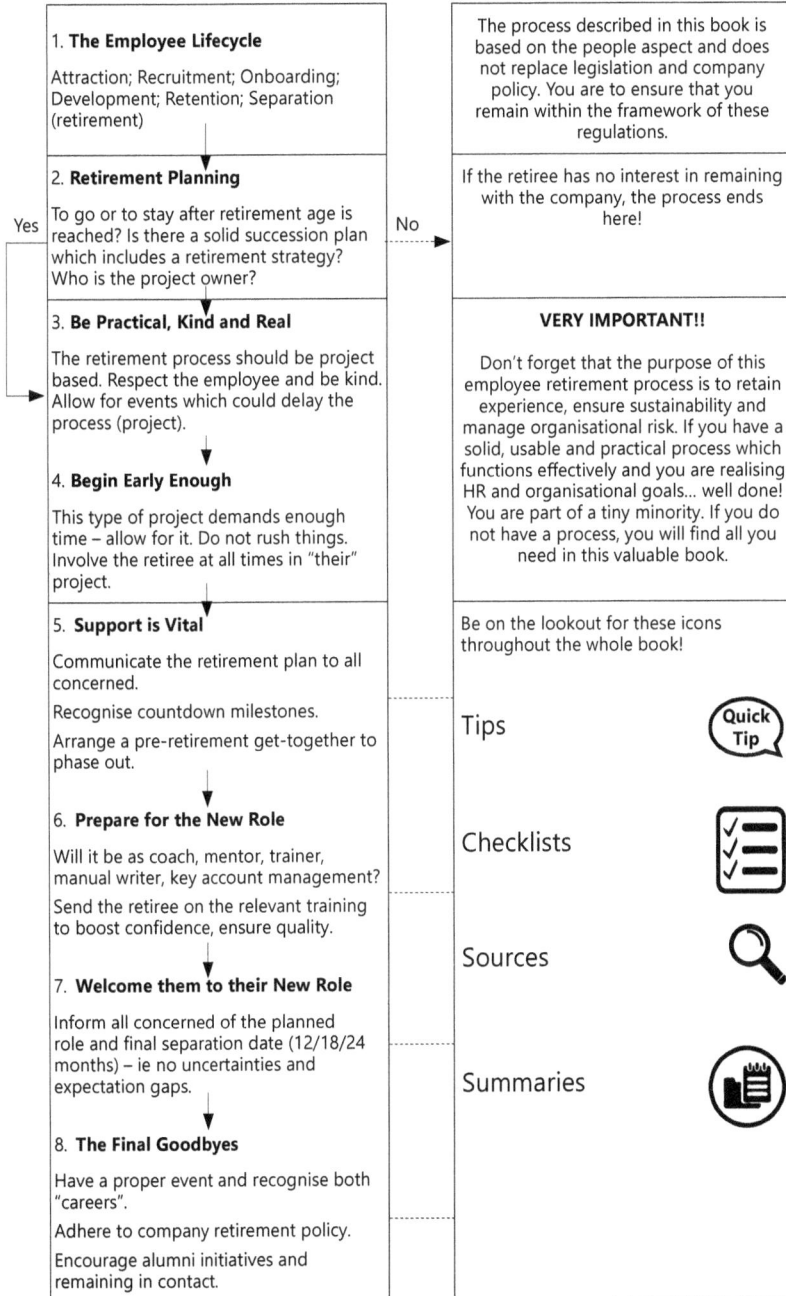

1. The Employee Lifecycle

Attraction; Recruitment; Onboarding; Development; Retention; Separation (retirement)

The process described in this book is based on the people aspect and does not replace legislation and company policy. You are to ensure that you remain within the framework of these regulations.

2. Retirement Planning

To go or to stay after retirement age is reached? Is there a solid succession plan which includes a retirement strategy? Who is the project owner?

Yes

No

If the retiree has no interest in remaining with the company, the process ends here!

3. Be Practical, Kind and Real

The retirement process should be project based. Respect the employee and be kind. Allow for events which could delay the process (project).

VERY IMPORTANT!!

Don't forget that the purpose of this employee retirement process is to retain experience, ensure sustainability and manage organisational risk. If you have a solid, usable and practical process which functions effectively and you are realising HR and organisational goals... well done! You are part of a tiny minority. If you do not have a process, you will find all you need in this valuable book.

4. Begin Early Enough

This type of project demands enough time – allow for it. Do not rush things. Involve the retiree at all times in "their" project.

5. Support is Vital

Communicate the retirement plan to all concerned.

Recognise countdown milestones.

Arrange a pre-retirement get-together to phase out.

Be on the lookout for these icons throughout the whole book!

Tips

Quick Tip

6. Prepare for the New Role

Will it be as coach, mentor, trainer, manual writer, key account management?

Send the retiree on the relevant training to boost confidence, ensure quality.

Checklists

7. Welcome them to their New Role

Inform all concerned of the planned role and final separation date (12/18/24 months) – ie no uncertainties and expectation gaps.

Sources

8. The Final Goodbyes

Have a proper event and recognise both "careers".

Adhere to company retirement policy.

Encourage alumni initiatives and remaining in contact.

Summaries

Chapter 1

The Employee Lifecycle

Welcome to the real deal!

The perfect orchestration of the symphony of life
is one of the Creator's greatest and most beautiful miracles.
Suzy Kassem

> **DID YOU KNOW?**
>
> *If you look after your employees, they will look after your business interest ... without being incentivised to do so.*

Introduction

The employee across the table from me was angry, really angry and it took me by surprise! The accusation caught me totally unawares, "So, am I no longer good enough?!"

Then it dawned on me...our planned chat about their retirement had triggered a flood of emotions that I was clearly not prepared for. The discussion ended well, albeit with some serious preoccupation on my part as to why this employee responded in this "negative" manner – after all, we all *know* that sooner or later we will be retiring. The reality only hits home, it seems, when an employee is actually faced with the actual event now being entered in a calendar.

This experience during my tenure as Human Resources Director of a large company was the catalyst for the development and use of a most rewarding and valuable programme – Preparing Employees for Retirement.

Background

The diagram below very nicely shows the process of finding suitable employees, training and motivating them, and then preparing them for retirement; this process is generally known as the *employee lifecycle*. Our focus in this book is on the "Wish me farewell" phase marked with a red circle.

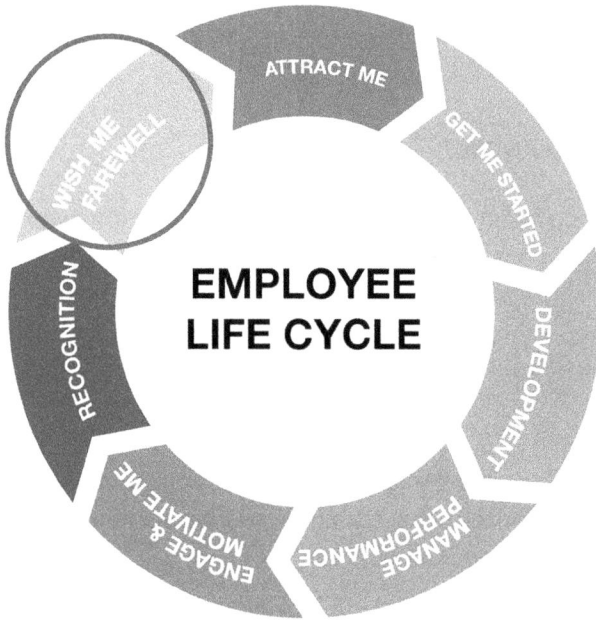

Figure 1: The employee lifecycle[1]

The question that most commonly came up while discussions about retirement were underway, was: "What do I do when I retire?"For the purpose of this talent-management guide and more specifically, *Preparing Employees for Retirement*, other questions are also dealt with, namely: how, when and in some cases, where...

In an article by Kathryn Tuggle[2], there are five hard things about retirement you were not expecting. One of these is key to our discussion in this book and that is "You realise that a large part of your identity was associated with your work."

"Men in particular get their identities wrapped up in what they do for a living, and once that's gone, if there's not something else there to fill the space, that's when the depression and dissatisfaction kicks in," Arnett says. People who are willing to sit down and discuss their passions and long-term post-retirement goals are the ones who will have a more satisfied, fulfilling retirement. "You can't just leave work and say, 'Oh, I'll figure it out,'" Arnett adds.

Without the human interaction and challenges found at the office, some people suffer mentally and physically, Olavsrud says. If you're not working, you may not be engaging in conversation with people on a daily basis or getting enough physical exercise. "You have to be cautious that you're still getting out, meeting people and being social," he says. "People who are not active tend to decline rather quickly."

To establish a routine and life goals, Olavsrud recommends connecting with a community association or other social or religious organisations of your choice. "What is going to motivate you to get out of bed and do something?" he asks. "For everyone it's going to be different, but you have to have something that motivates you, excites you and keeps you moving forward."

One study published in the *Journal of Epidemiology and Community Health* found that working for one additional year after age 65 was associated with an 11% lower risk of mortality, leading researchers to suggest that "prolonged working life may provide survival benefits among US adults".

Research also suggests a job you don't like can still be better than no job at all. "Even disliked colleagues and a bad boss are better than social isolation because they can provide cognitive challenges that keep the mind active and healthy," according to an article published by the National Bureau of Economic Research.

It is possible to keep your brain active and to maintain social connections in retirement, but it becomes a lot harder without the workplace to provide you with a ready-made source of human contact and mental challenges.[3]

There is an immense amount of onboarding and employee satisfaction information available on the internet, social media and repositories around the globe, but far less information about preparing employees for retirement. This book will hopefully help plug this gap and provide some very useful and practical information on the topic.

It is useful to bear in mind the fact that people spend a lot of time and effort (and money!) on planning and getting that top job; then they spend even more time and effort getting better and earning more or being entrusted with ever more responsibility and then... BAM! all of a sudden some (usually younger) employee is telling them they are going to retire quite soon! Of course, this is not going to be easy for them to process, accept and then turn the retirement into something positive. The author is confident that the information, tips and experiences shared in this valuable book will make the process a lot easier and simpler for both the departing employee as well as the employer.

The legal side of things

The laws of the land, as applicable to all types of employees, as well as industry and company guidelines, policies and procedures, dictate what companies should do in order to ensure the wellbeing, safety, health and productivity of a country's employed citizens. Although from time to time reference to legal requirements is made in this book, readers are to be aware that its purpose is not to clarify legislative requirements or to seek to assist in the compliance with company policy. For this reason, please note that at all times, it is explicitly stated that all retirement-related policies, procedures and processes take place within the legislative stipulations of the employer as well as the country. Furthermore, no financial aspects and/or planning matters are covered – these are best dealt with by a certified financial planner.

Quick Tip

Obtain written approval prior commencement,
for retirement plans from the company's legal department.

The good news!

There are some really easy and worthwhile ways to make the retirement process really workable, fair and productive – some examples are shown below to help you make the most of this important phase of an employee's lifecycle. If you already have sound policies and procedures in place in your company and you are successfully retaining experience by means of positive employee retirement preparation, then this guide will be the cherry on top, offering solid advice and a really good example of how this process is correctly done!

One of these ways is to check out what other companies that have really good retirement plans are offering. A good source is, for example, The Top Employers Institute[1] which offers a certification programme that enables organisations to assess and improve the workplace environment; this includes retirement practices and procedures. An annual competition is held, the Top Employers are announced and the winner's details are available on the Top Employers Institute website.

Another, very useful source is to speak to the South Africa Board of People Practice (SABPP) or the Institute of People Management (IPM) and ask them for pointers in this regard. Both these entities have a lot of data on people management matters and should be able to offer some direction and/or advice.

---

[1] The Top Employers Institute (www. Top-employers.com) is the global authority on recognising excellence in people practices. Established more than 25 years ago, the Top Employers Institute has certified over 1 500 organisations in 118 countries/regions. These Certified Top Employers positively impact the lives of over 6 000 000 employees globally.

The third way to find some references is to speak to colleagues, friends and family and enquire whether they know or know of a person about to retire or who has recently retired and to have a chat to these people.

The best news is that, by reading (and working through) this book, you will be able to design, plan and execute a retirement best-practice operating procedure that will serve you and your organisation very well.

Conclusion

As we move on to Chapter 2, it is hoped that this guide will open up avenues of new thinking, improved people management practices and give rise to the establishment of a great, fresh way of dealing with your most precious and valuable asset – your people!

With step one now behind us, let's move on to step 2! For convenience's sake, a linear "compass" is shown at the end of each chapter to help the reader keep track and to follow the golden thread of this book.

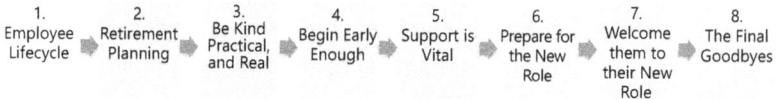

1. Employee Lifecycle	2. Retirement Planning	3. Be Kind Practical, and Real	4. Begin Early Enough	5. Support is Vital	6. Prepare for the New Role	7. Welcome them to their New Role	8. The Final Goodbyes

Summary of Chapter 1: The Employee Lifecycle

1. Be prepared to change.
2. Read with thought.
3. Apply project management principles to ease the implementation.
4. Don't be scared to ask questions.
5. Trust the process.
6. Share each step of the plan with the retiring employee.

Chapter 2

Retirement Planning

To Go or not to Go; that is the question!

It is paradoxical that the idea of living a long life appeals to everyone,
but the idea of getting old doesn't appeal to anyone.
Andy Rooney

> **DID YOU KNOW?**
> *There are currently 3.9 million Baby Boomers in South Africa.*[4]

Introduction

The topic of manpower and/or labour planning is one which features
quite often and quite highly in most Human Resources departments,
in one way or the other. However, featuring does not necessarily
imply any action has been taken – it too often merely implies that
the matter has been discussed, a most impressive report has been
submitted, and a tick has been made in the box! In this chapter we
will discuss what to do to ensure that workforce planning (especially
as it relates to retirees) is executed in a structured, fair and timeous
manner, and that value is retained.

There is no standard or benchmark to use as reference when
an enterprise is contemplating the retirement of one or more
employees. It is very much a matter of what the legal ramifications
are, what is best for the company (usually) at the time of retirement
and whether the decision is employee-lifecycle driven or whether
the organisation is cutting costs by reducing staff numbers. It
is therefore, very important that the company strategy, via the
Human Resources Strategy, informs the retirement process so that
organisational objectives are actually achieved. The risk of retirement

programmes not being informed by organisational strategy is that the programme is not dealt with in the appropriate manner and with the attention it deserves, or that the retirement of a particular employee, or group of employees, is cynically considered by fellow workers as the company making a feeble attempt to cut costs by getting rid of the "old people!"

The following article, "Retiring employees: 8 tips for a smooth transition"[5] very nicely explains the approach one could take:

Many organisations are facing a worrisome situation – retirement looms for a large percentage of their workforce and younger workers aren't yet ready to fill those shoes. What strategies can you implement to proactively preserve the wealth of institutional knowledge that drives your company's productivity?

Here are eight tips to help soon-to-be-retiring employees make a smooth exit:

1. **Avoid knowledge silos**

    Long-time employees have often formed relationships across the company, giving them a deeper understanding of how their job impacts someone else's work in another area. If your company's policies or procedures don't actively encourage knowledge-sharing across departments, silos can result. Without a broader appreciation for other departmental roles, younger, less experienced employees may unwittingly sow chaos, causing delays or costly mistakes.

    To avoid such silos, encourage managers to have experienced employees share their knowledge in monthly meetings, or document the bare bones of processes and procedures particular to them.

2. **Don't undervalue older workers**

    Many companies make the mistake of thinking younger, less experienced employees will cost less than older employees who make more money. Beware the younger, cheaper siren call.

Long-time employees have built a wealth of knowledge about how to work most efficiently and know your customers. They know what's worked in the past, what hasn't, and why. A younger, less experienced employee, eager to make their mark, may implement policies and procedures that have failed numerous times before, alienating customers and costing the company money.

Also, avoid signalling to senior employees that you want them to leave by asking, "Are you ready to retire?" A subtler conversation may begin with, "What are your plans for the next three to five years?"

3. Cross-train employees

Cross-training is another antidote to the brain-drain inherent when long-time employees leave. A three- to six-month assignment in another department allows younger or newer workers to gain hands-on experience in areas of the company unfamiliar to them. Cross-training can also build your operational team and prevent information silos.

To prevent older workers from feeling threatened, be sure to communicate that the purpose of cross-training is to build company-wide knowledge, not to push senior staff out the door.

4. Consider alternatives to full retirement

Some employees want to start their permanent vacation ASAP. Others may want to remain in a part-time or consulting role for a few years before hopping in their RV and riding into the sunset. For these employees, such alternative work arrangements offer reduced stress and a continued, though smaller, paycheck.

For employers, part-timers can lessen the chaos caused by a sudden change in personnel. Going part-time forces needed changes in roles and responsibilities, but leaves the older worker in place and available to answer questions and share wisdom.

Occasional consulting may work for special projects or to free an experienced manager to coach newer leaders.

5. Plan succession across all departments

Succession plans aren't just for the C-suite. You also need to pay attention to whether an entire department is closing in on retirement, and manage accordingly.

For instance, if your entire HR department is 55+, you have trouble brewing. As older HR workers retire or make lateral moves, you should have a plan in place so that younger specialists and managers have time to learn from their older peers and become ready to step into senior roles when the time comes.

Some managers unconsciously get into the mind-set of thinking they need someone of a particular age, gender or other external characteristic rather than focusing on skill set.

A succession plan that outlines each position's key roles and responsibilities can help an organisation shake such self-limiting behaviours and create opportunities to find excellent replacements for retiring workers. Remember, someone's style or work cadence doesn't necessarily equate with an ability to learn or fulfil a new role.

6. Manage across generations

Aging employees need to know that it's part of their job to train the younger generation, and younger workers need to know it's their job to learn from their more experienced peers. At the same time, you don't want to signal to older workers that their experience is unappreciated or unneeded, or that you think it's time for them to leave. You can help facilitate cross-generational learning by reminding everyone that there is much to be learned from different perspectives and work styles. Often, if the leader fosters an open-sharing work environment it can minimise feelings of ageism or discrimination that older workers may feel as they begin to transition.

An open environment can be as simple or complex as the leader desires. It may take the form of quarterly team huddles. For a younger manager, showing respect to older workers might mean planning a staff outing to a museum rather than a rock-climbing facility. For an older manager, it might mean encouraging senior staff to mentor a younger employee or engaging them in the process of planning for their retirement.

7.   Make annual assessments

Whether it's succession planning or knowledge sharing, you should conduct a retirement assessment annually. Take a look at which departments or jobs may be heavy on soon-to-retire employees. Have conversations with your long-time employees and ask, "What do you do that's not in your job description? How do you do it?"

Tenured employees are often the ones who've created bypasses for broken or inefficient processes – processes you may not know are broken. Such conversations give you the opportunity to capture what these workers know and use it to the company's advantage.

8.   Don't wait till they're out the door

Knowledge transfer takes time and effort, so don't wait until a week before the retirement party to start the process. Either through mentorship, job sharing, job shadowing or other techniques, have your retiring workers share the whys behind what they do and the way they do it.

If you ask someone to document their job, it doesn't have to be terribly formal or in-depth, but it should cover the key elements. They should identify those processes that are critical to the business, including important details, such as where files are kept.

It signals an appreciation for what your aging employees do when you ask them to Buddy with you in planning their graceful exit.

In the end, always go back to the human element when dealing with someone's retirement. Remember, you are touching on this person's livelihood and their identity, so proceed with kindness and respect.

Quick Tip

Ensure that any retirement actions are included in the company succession plan, or you may end up with conflicting points of view and risk losing the credibility of the process.

A company's strategic intent and subsequent plan to attract and retain the best talent, will not be complete if it does not include succession planning. Unfortunately, many succession plans remain just that – a *plan* which is not implemented, maintained and used, other than to serve as proof that the organisation actually has a succession plan.

So, what should a succession plan consist of and how does it actually work?

A visit to any internet search engine for the phrase "succession plans" reveals about 62 million results! There is therefore no shortage on data, information, plans, ideas, arguments, theories etc. about succession and/or succession planning. The real challenge for any leadership team is to decide on the most suitable strategy for the succession planning, select the most appropriate plan and then customise the action plan or standard operating procedures to best suit the enterprise's customer base, industry and culture. Experience has shown, again and again, that by being inclusive and including multiple hierarchical levels, as well as various company subject matter experts, new organisational initiatives have a far bigger chance of surviving beyond the launch event with its beautiful photographs and delicious snacks!

With that being stated, most companies have succession planning incorporated into their Human Resources plan as well as on the risk register (it is very important to be aware of the risk factor when discussing talent retention).

Table 2 is an example of a simple succession plan worksheet. Readers are to bear in mind that this example is very basic, however it can be used until the specific organisational plan has evolved into something more suitable.

Table 1: Completed Succession Planning Worksheet (Courtesy CHP HR Services)[6]

Position Title	Incumbent Name	Retirement Status	Criticality	Number of Staff Ready Now	Number of Staff Ready in 1-2 Years	Succession Planning Priorities
CEO		A	1	1	1	
CHRO			1	0	0	x
COO		B	1	0	2	x
CFO		A	1	1	2	
CTO		C	2	0	1	
CRO		B	2	0	0	
Technical Dir.		A	1	2	3	
Payroll Mngr.		C	2	1	2	
Personnel			2	1	1	
L&D Mngr.		B	2	2	2	
Ops. Mngr. 1			1	0	0	x
Ops. Mngr. 2		A	1	0	1	x
Operator 1		C	2	0	1	x

Retirement Status: A: Retirement likely within 1 year B: Retirement likely within 3 years C: Retirement eligible within 5 years	**Criticality:** 1: Critical – Must "hit the ground running" 2: Very Important – Fully functional within 6 months

The actual plan would look something like the following example borrowed from an internal source.

Table 2: Succession Plan example

1. Communicate Possible Opportunities	2. Identify Who Is Interested
■ Inform employees of the possible job opportunities that are anticipated over the designated time period (e.g., next three years). ■ Communicate what key competencies are needed for those jobs. That is, what level of demonstrated skills and knowledge is management looking for in potential candidates for these jobs? ■ Inform employees of the succession planning process that the organisation intends to use (e.g., the steps in this model).	■ Open it up. Give employees the opportunity to indicate interest in possible job openings and willingness to participate in succession planning activities. Clarify that participation in succession planning is not a guarantee of advancement. However, participation could help one's chances.
3. Assess Competency Readiness	**4. Prepare Development Plans**
■ Assess individuals' readiness to assume possible job openings for which they have indicated interest. ■ That is, compare the employee's present competency level to that required of the anticipated opening. Identify competencies that need development to help ready the employee for that job or occupation. It is advisable to use an assessment instrument that actively engages the employee as well as the supervisor in determining the employee's competency levels.	■ Together with the employee, prepare an individual development plan that outlines specific activities that the employee engages in to develop needed competencies. Include a timetable with milestones for assessing progress. ■ The list of activities and timetable should be reflected in the employee's EDPP. ■ In addition to individual plans, it may make sense to have a group development plan applicable to core competencies for a particular occupation level that all interested employees should participate in. Consultation in preparing training plans and determining appropriate activities is available through the Department of Personnel's Training & Development Services.

5. Provide Development Opportunities	6. Formalise Eligibility

▓ Help the employee follow through with the development plan by setting up training options and providing realistic time to participate in the training activities indicated in the employee's development plan.
 	
▓ The employee should also take personal responsibility to take the initiative and seek out activities that will help develop the targeted competencies. This display of initiative and follow-through can show that the employee is serious about succession and may, in itself, be a key competency.
 	
Training options go well beyond the traditional classroom setting and do not have to be costly. Examples of development activities include: mentoring, job shadowing, task force participation, special projects/assignments, Internet and journal research, conferences, time-limited job rotations, video/audio tapes, committee participation, etc.
	▓ For general service classified positions, employees typically must get on the appropriate job register to be formally eligible.
	
	▓ Avenues to increase flexibility to formalise eligibility include:
	  ▫ Use "until further notice" recruitment announcements so that employees can submit their application at any time
	  ▫ Use desirable, not minimum, qualifications
	  ▫ Streamline selection procedures – avoid using complicated multiple-choice exams.
	  ▫ Use the "in-training" programme that allows bringing the employee in at a lower level with automatic advancement to the higher level.
	  ▫ Use competency-based classification structures.
	
	For WMS and exempt positions, hiring procedures are flexible and established by the hiring agency.

The Buddy System and Onboarding of New Employees

This book would not be complete, if we did not discuss the career path, or journey, of the successor, who in all likelihood will be a new recruit. And of course, every new employee should be properly inducted and be made to feel welcome and to understand how the company functions. The onboarding guide below may prove to be very useful especially considering that, 61 percent of new hires do not get any training on company culture. (TalentLMS). Introducing new employees to the company culture is one of the main points covered during the onboarding process.

A new employee's onboarding is greatly enhanced by assigning an office Buddy, a fellow employee (other than the manager) who provides advice and guidance on the different aspects of working at the company. A Buddy is also a "sounding board" who offers encouragement as the new employee acclimates to the company's culture and workplace.

Selection Criteria and Process

The successful Buddy is an employee who fully understands the company's culture and environment (has been employed at the company for at least one year) and wants to be a Buddy.

Additional criteria include:

- Time to be accessible and available to the employee.
- Familiar with employee's role and work unit.
- A solid performer.
- Strong communication and interpersonal skills.
- Exemplifies the company's values.
- Patience and empathy.
- Well regarded and trusted by others.

Individuals can volunteer to be considered as a Buddy or recommended by others. Local Human Resources and/or the hiring manager can make the final choice based on the selection criteria.

Buddy Responsibilities

In assisting a new employee acclimating to the company, a Buddy serves as a valuable resource by creating a trusting relationship and maintaining confidentiality.

Responsibilities include:

- Providing information on policies and procedures.
- Identifying resources in the workplace.
- Familiarising the employee with the company's culture, norms, and unwritten guidelines.
- Introducing the employee to others in the unit and throughout the company.
- Taking the employee on an expanded tour of the workplace and campus.
- Answering questions and referring the employee to the appropriate resources.

Suggested Structure

Ideally, there is a formal, six-month relationship between the Buddy and the new employee. Toward the end of the six months, they can discuss if and how to continue their relationship (perhaps as mentor) outside of the structured Buddy role. On the employee's first or second day, introduce the Buddy and employee. This introduction can be facilitated by your local HR or the hiring manager. Discuss the Buddy's role and responsibilities as well as the employee's needs, and answer any questions. Ensure that the Buddy and employee meet during the first week (ideally for breakfast or lunch, if possible). Suggest and then allow the Buddy and employee to decide on the frequency, length, topics, and method of interaction between the two of them. The structure will vary. What's important is that the arrangement is clearly defined and works for both the employee and the Buddy. Here is one of many possible examples:

Week 1:
- Meet for an hour (over breakfast or lunch, if possible).
- Learn about each other's background, experience, interests, etc.
- Decide on the most important and relevant things to cover.

- Respond to any immediate questions the employee may have.

- Agree on frequency, length and method of communication.

Months 1 and 2:

- Meet weekly for a half hour (in person).

- Be available for phone conversations and email.

- Take employee on a campus tour.

- Introduce employee to other colleagues.

Months 3 and 4:

- Meet bi-weekly for a half hour (mix of in person and by phone).

- Be available for phone conversations and email.

- Have a check-in with employee, and local HR and hiring manager.

- Invite employee to relevant company business or social events, and introduce him/her to others.

Months 5 and 6:

- Meet monthly for an hour (in person).

- Continue introducing employee to colleagues and inviting employee to relevant business or social events.

- Decide if and how to continue the Buddy relationship. Have a wrap-up with employee, HR, and hiring manager.

Liz Ryan, CEO of Human Workplace, compiled a very simple, yet ever so useful list of 10 good things to give a new employee; I suggest you do something similar.

1. *A cheat sheet with coworkers' names, extensions, email addresses, IM handles and job titles.*

2. *A simple org chart.*

3.   *A list of contacts for payroll, benefits and other common issues.*

4.   *A mug (premade with their name printed on it).*

5.   *A calendar of company holidays.*

6.   *A glossary of company/industry terms with definitions.*

7.   *A welcome card signed by their coworkers.*

8.   *A list of the company's and department's top goals for the year.*

9.   *A logo tchotchke (squeeze ball, lanyard, etc.).*

10. *What would you add?*

Note: HR and/or the line manager is responsible for having a mid-point check-in and a wrap-up conversation with the employee and Buddy.

With the onboarding now suitably dealt with for purposes of this book, it is very important in this phase of ERP to appoint the responsible person or project owner. I quite like the title of "project owner" because it signifies that there is a beginning and an end to, in this case ERP, and that the project will be given the focus and budget it deserves. It may be a good idea to inform all stakeholders who the ERP Project Manager is so that any questions or requests may be directed to the correct champion/process owner.

With an assessment or audit (an assessment sounds less intimidating!) now done and dusted, one can confidently prepare the respective (and correct) candidate for their departure in a properly planned and dignified manner. Is this employee, after all, not one of many who helped build and grow the company to what it is at the time of their impending retirement? Do not forget that...

Now... what if the retiring employee does not *want* to stay on? Then one follows the exact same process minus the post-retirement role and one ensures that the employee departs with confidence and dignity.

1. Employee Lifecycle	➡	2. Retirement Planning	➡	3. Be Kind Practical, and Real	➡	4. Begin Early Enough	➡	5. Support is Vital	➡	6. Prepare for the New Role	➡	7. Welcome them to their New Role	➡	8. The Final Goodbyes

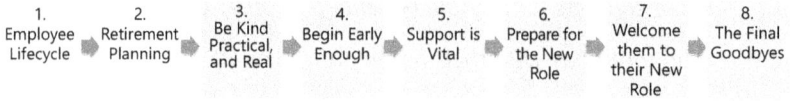

Summary of Chapter 2: Retirement Planning

1. Update your HR plan and labour demand matrix.

2. Is your company strategy and HR strategy aligned and current?

3. Ensure that your HR plan, succession plan and exit plan are aligned.

4. Check that you are working within the legal guidelines.

5. Communicate the progress to all the relevant stakeholders.

Chapter 3

Be Practical, Kind and Real

Let's get started!

Carry out a random act of kindness, with no expectation of reward,
safe in the knowledge that one day someone might do the same for you.
Princess Diana

> **DID YOU KNOW?**
> *During the next 20 years, 10,000 people in South Africa will turn
> 65 every day.[7]*

Introduction

In spite of many global shortages, famine and too little of this and
too little of that, the one thing that is in abundance, is information.
Just about every person I know and everyone I have spoken to,
about coping and stress-related matters, have one thing in common
– information overload! There is so much information flooding
electronic devices all over the world that it is overwhelming and,
eventually, irritating. Amongst all of this information is a plethora of
theories and self-help guides written by passionate people, mostly
wanting to make life a bit easier and earn a few bucks while doing it.

So, what is the point?

The point is, that with so much theoretical advice floating
around, it is very easy to fall into a state of confusion, apathy and
indecisiveness. This book you have in your hands now, will greatly
assist in helping you get started very easily in a most practical way
and allow you to execute a great retirement preparation plan with
very little effort and stress.

To set the scene for this chapter, all about being pragmatic, I will share a humbling and beautiful personal experience relating to practical succession and retirement planning. Peter was an ambitious employee who had worked his way up to the level of Senior Supervisor over quite a few years. Barriers and setbacks did not deter him from becoming a most knowledgeable, skilful and likeable fellow with a sound track record. He had been nominated by his manager, Daniel, an operations manager, to be the operations manager's successor in due course. Back at the HR department, Peter was listed as Daniel's successor and Peter's training was intensified, his work performance was evaluated and in general, the "watch-this-guy-grow" expression was very often used in the context of Peter's Personal Development Plan (PDP).

As time went by, Peter was noticed by a client and, as is sadly so often the case, was duly approached and offered an operations manager position at almost double the salary! Daniel was not happy and insisted that Peter has been "poached"... (As any savvy manager will know, "poaching" is merely a euphemism for explaining that the current employer did not adequately value the employee and that the employee resigned!) During Peter's exit interview he was most surprised to learn that he had been nominated by his manager as a successor; Daniel had never bothered to tell Peter that he was valued, that his excellent performance had been noticed and that he was officially on the company's succession plan!

Now is the best time to get started with our easy-to-use, practical and most rewarding ERP. And the opportunity to leave a legacy for a long, long time. After all, people remember *how* you make them feel long after they have forgotten *what* you did for them.

As most people know, the best results usually emanate from good plans and good plans almost always stem from lots and lots of thinking. A stack of thinking and planning has been done for you and you can enjoy that feeling of having found an authentic and credible short-cut to your programme that is arranged in a useful A-B-C format.

A. DOCUMENT CHECK

First of all, one should check that the following company documents exist, are up to date, accessible and actually being used in the correct manner. Where quality management systems like ISO are in use, it should be relatively quick and easy to acquire this information. If there is no formal quality management system in place, this checklist can be a useful guide to get some form of quality management system in place; at least in the Human Resources department. Please note that this list is not considered the ultimate list – company industry, policy and many other factors will influence this list and may result in more or less documents. For the purposes of the topic of this book and to ensure proper alignment throughout the enterprise, a shorter list may be inadequate to ensure a smooth and efficient employee retirement plan (ERP). The ERP process is also known as Phased Retirement and some additional international information will be shared as an additional resource to assist you in preparing the best ERP possible.

	Document Name	Yes/No
1	Company Strategy	
2	Company Organisational Chart (Organogram)	
3	Human Resources Strategy	
4	Company HR Plan	
5	National Skills Plan	
6	Sector Skills Plan	
7	Workplace Skills Plan	
9	Annual Training Report	
10	Employment Equity Plan	
11	Career Path Plan	
12	Personal Development Plans	

Once this check has been done, it may be useful to cast an eye over a typical ERP policy. At this point it may be useful to include some international Phased Retirement literature.[8]

"Just like the name sounds, phased retirement is a gradual step down from full-time work to part-time work to full retirement, spreading out the change over time to make it easier for both parties – the retiree and the organisation – to transition."

New Call-to-Action

So, in this guide, we will explore some phased retirement best practices while also looking at the benefits of implementing a phased retirement solution alongside some of the possible downsides.

First, What is Phased Retirement?

Like we mentioned above, phased retirement is a process used to help employees gradually exit the workforce while also allowing the company they are leaving the time they need to find a suitable replacement.

"Phased Retirement is a human resources tool that allows full-time employees to work part-time schedules while beginning to draw retirement benefits," writes the US Office of Personnel Management (OPM).

"This new tool will allow managers to better provide unique mentoring opportunities for employees while increasing access to the decades of institutional knowledge and experience that retirees can provide."

This gradual step down happens in – as the name suggests – phases. Phased retirement plans can differ from organisation to organisation or person to person. However, there are laws that mandate how older workers are treated and we strongly suggest you read up on them or consult your legal team before implementing a policy of your own.

That doesn't mean you can't be creative with your phased retirement policy – you just have to make sure you follow the rules and aren't discriminating.

Okay, now that we have a baseline understanding of what phased retirement is, let's get into the major benefits of the programme.

The Benefits of Phased Retirement

Today's workforce is in a state of flux because there are more generations working right now than ever before. We have Gen Z making their workforce entrance, Millennials settling in, Gen X entering upper management, and Baby Boomers making their exit.

This presents a few problems, namely that Baby Boomers are hitting retirement age en masse. There's a commonly stated stat that proclaims that about 10,000 Baby Boomers hit retirement age every day in the US. That means that they are now eligible for retirement.

Despite the fact that retirement is changing – Boomers are working far longer than other generations who reach retirement age – the fact remains that Boomers are starting to make a big exit from the workforce, taking a lot of their skills, knowledge, and proven leadership skills with them.

So, in order to curb the negative effects of the this sudden exit, Human Resources needs to find a way to transfer all of those skills to Gen Xers and Millennials who will be filling in the role. Phased retirement can seriously help with this because it allows the retiree to slowly reduce their workload while teaching those who will remain.

Knowledge transfer can keep a business rolling through all of these transitions. It also helps deal with a side of retirement that we typically ignore.

Quick Tip

Do some sound boarding with colleagues in your industry and learn what works and what possibly, does not.

Understanding the Hidden Side of Retirement

Like we said up top, retirement conversations are dominated by financial discussions. When we first enter the workforce, we're told over and over that we need to start saving for our eventual retirement.

While this is good advice – you obviously do need to have a nest egg ready for when you make the switch – we tend to ignore the social, emotional, and personal side of retirement. What are we supposed to do with all of our newfound free time? Will I still see all of my friends?

These questions are common yet there are rarely plans in place to help employees through their retirement lifestyle planning. This makes them not want to retire, which can become problematic for employers and is obviously a huge bummer for retirees who have worked their entire lives for a chance to retire.

So, with a phased retirement programme, retirees can slowly make the switch instead of abruptly changing their entire lives. This also helps employers reduce the risk of 'brain drain' that can happen when multiple people decide to retire at one time.

With that in mind, what are the benefits of having a knowledge transfer plan?

Future Proofing Your Workforce

When retirees leave, they can take time-honed expertise with them, leaving younger workers struggling to fulfil the role.

"Knowing who knows what, who needs to know what, and how to transfer that knowledge is critical – especially when so much of a company's worth consists of information," says Chris Cancialosi in an article for *Forbes*. "Investing in developing an effective way to transfer knowledge may, in the least, save you some headaches and, at the most, save your business."

Cancialosi says that knowledge transfer starts when a person is hired. You need to make sure that you have a plan to train that person and infuse them with the knowledge of their leaders so that when it comes time to take over, they can do so without any headaches.

Phased retirement plans offer this training, though if you want to do it well, a knowledge transfer plan needs to be put on paper long before a retiree starts the exit process.

By knowing what knowledge you need to retain and how you will retain it, you will be able to help the retiree understand and prepare for the hidden side of retirement while knowing that you already have a plan for your business to continue without them.

Also, according to numerous HR leaders, workforce planning is a hugely competitive advantage for organisations to employ. However, most HR teams neglect workforce planning because it never seems like the right time to make a plan.

B. POLICY DOCUMENT[9]

Retirement policy example

Introduction: Retirement is an important transition for both the departing employee and the organisation. A well-planned retirement policy will save you time and grief in the long run.

This document provides a structured approach to developing a retirement policy and includes the following elements:

- Early and phased retirement procedures.
- Notification requirements.
- Role transition.

Policy Title	*Retirement Policy*
Policy Owner	*Human Resources*
Policy Approver(s)	*CHRO, HRD*
Effective Date	*List the date that this policy went into effect.*
Next Review Date	*List the date that this policy must undergo review and update.*

Purpose: [Organisation name] strives to make the transition from employment to retirement as smooth as possible. This policy governs retirement procedures for all employees. Note that [organisation name] has no mandatory retirement age and retirement age refers to the age at which we will support an employee to retire to be eligible for retirement options.

Scope: This policy applies to all [full-time, part-time; insert other groups if necessary] employees. Eligibility for Retirement: In accordance with applicable laws and regulations employees are not required to retire at the end of the month in which they turn [insert age, e.g. 65].

Early Retirement Procedures: Employees who have reached 55 [or specify age] years of age are eligible for early retirement with a pension (if a pension is provided) and benefits (if provided) reduced for early retirement. All retirement applications must include the desired date of retirement. Employees are advised that all applications for retirement will be considered on a case-by-case basis with a view to balance [organisation name]'s business objectives and the employee's wishes. If an employee's application is not approved, Human Resources [or specify position] will meet with the employee to discuss the reasons for the decision and arrive at a mutually satisfactory agreement.

Phased Retirement: *Use this section to document your organisation's early retirement procedures. Sample Procedures: Retiring employees [in the following groups: (list groups)] have the option of phasing out of their position by gradually reducing their workload. The maximum length of the phasing period is two [or insert suitable period] years leading up to the retirement date. Employees wishing to take advantage of this option are required to meet with Human Resources and the head of their department to develop a mutually satisfactory phase-out plan and ensure that succession planning requirements are met for the employee's position. Employees who choose the phased retirement option will retain all benefits and privileges with the exceptions of the following items, which are based on full-time status or time worked:*

■ *Paid vacation time and leaves based on time worked.*

■ *Medical benefits based on full-time status.*

Procedures and Responsibilities Notice of Retirement:. *Employees are required to provide a minimum of 12 [or insert another period] months' notice of retirement to accommodate the transition and knowledge transfer processes.The notice must be made in writing and submitted to [Human Resources and the employee's immediate manager]. Although Human Resources will notify employees of their eligibility for retirement no later than 12 months before their [65th, or insert relevant age] birthday, it is the employee's responsibility to provide notice of their chosen date of retirement in accordance with the above timeline.*

Property: *All [organisation name] property will be handed over by the retiring employee in accordance with the Offboarding Policy [or specify relevant policy]. If the retiring employee chooses to remain with [organisation name] on a part-time contract Human Resources and IT will make and document appropriate equipment and access arrangements.*

Role Transition: As part of [organisation name] succession planning programme, role transition plans will be developed for [list positions and/or employee groups] to facilitate the transition process and transfer of knowledge. Human Resources and managers will develop individual transition plans for each retiring employee included in the succession planning programme.
The plans will include:

- Accountabilities and expectations for the departing employee, their successor, and manager.
- Knowledge transfer requirements, methods, and timeline.
- The retiring employee's alternative work arrangements, if applicable.
- [Insert other items if applicable].

The following are the most commonly used knowledge transfer methods:

- Mentoring.
- Job shadowing.
- Special assignments.
- [Insert method not covered elsewhere].

All enquiries about the development of an appropriate transition plan should be directed to Human Resources [or insert specific position if available]. Note that if an employee has retired and is hired-back on a full or part time contract or contingent basis the employee (will or will not) be eligible for additional benefits offered to employees.

All benefits provided by [organisation name] will cease on the date of an employee's retirement with the exception of the following (specify any provision for benefits including insurance, dental and medical to continue after retirement and what, if any, money an employee must pay to remain part of the benefits package). Retiring employee will receive payouts for any earned vacation that has not been taken on the date of their retirement.

*Employee Declaration:*I, [Name, Surname] hereby acknowledge that I have read and understand [organisation name]'s Retirement Policy. I agree to abide by the terms and conditions of this policy and ensure that persons working under my supervision abide by the terms and conditions of this policy. I understand that if I violate or fail to comply with this policy, I may face legal or disciplinary action according to applicable laws or [organisation name] policies.

_____   _____

Employee Signature Date   Manager Signature Date

SELECT THE ELIGIBLE EMPLOYEES

The Lexico Dictionary defines selection as, "The action or fact of carefully choosing someone or something as being the best or most suitable."[10] Sadly, in many cases, factors like for example, prejudice, nepotism and discrimination result in the best people being overlooked or ignored and a "more suitable" person being retained. This must not and cannot happen! Eligibility is another great word for the state of having the right to do or obtain something through satisfaction of the appropriate conditions.[11] When considering the eligibility of an employee for retirement, it is most important to ensure that minimum requirements are not overshadowed by subjectivity or any other factors which aggravate the situation unnecessarily.

By now, I am sure you will agree, it is extremely important that fairness, transparency and healthy dialogue are followed in order to do what is best for the organisation as well as the individual.

| 1. Employee Lifecycle | 2. Retirement Planning | 3. Be Kind Practical, and Real | 4. Begin Early Enough | 5. Support is Vital | 6. Prepare for the New Role | 7. Welcome them to their New Role | 8. The Final Goodbyes |

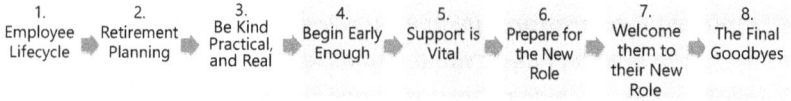

Summary of Chapter 3: Be Practical, Kind and Real

1. Use all the information you have access to.

2. Phased retirement does not drive itself, you must!

3. Future-proof your organisation by retaining experienced talent.

4. Be fair and transparent when selecting a suitable person.

5. Be prepared to make some adaptions to legacy practices.

Chapter 4

Begin Early Enough

Time waits for no one!

Mother Teresa reminds us that, "Yesterday is gone.
Tomorrow has not yet come.
We have only today. Let us begin."
This wisdom is also applicable to preparing employees for
retirement – one should not waste time and run the risk of missing
opportunities and forfeiting some excellent human potential
development rewards.

> **DID YOU KNOW?**
> *The second biggest regret people who retired have is leaving the
> workforce too early and not staying busy. The first is not having
> saved enough money.* (www.cheatsheet.com)

Introduction

Before rushing off to find a suitable programme or some toolkit to
assist in the planning, here is some good news: just apply good old
project management principles. The humblest of garden projects
right through to Elon Musk's rocket programme, all are project
managed so that a particular project starts and finishes on time
(ideally) and that progress is tracked accordingly. There is no reason
why your employee retirement programme should not also be
managed just like a project and be rewarded with success and joy all
round.

Let's jump right in and get this great programme going!

It may be useful to give a short background on exactly what project management is and how to use it – this will save a lot of time and bother later on. And, remember, we are talking about project management principles and disciplines, not a particular software programme or other expensive tools which add unnecessary cost to the ERP; an HRMS, Microsoft's Excel, Project and whichever calendar programme is used, are more than adequate. A calendar is an amazing tool if one has a structured and disciplined approach to life.

What is a project?

A project[12] is a temporary endeavour undertaken to create a unique product or service. 'Temporary' means that every project has a definite end. 'Unique' means that the product or service is different in some distinguishing way from all similar products or services. Other distinctive features of a project include:

- A **start and finish** (sometimes difficult to define – the start may have crystallised over a period of time and the end may be a slow phase-out).

- A **lifecycle** (a beginning and an end, with a number of distinct phases in between).

- A budget with an associated cashflow.

- Activities that are essentially unique and **non-repetitive.**

- Use of **resources** from different departments which need coordinating.

- A single point of responsibility (i.e. the project manager) in this case; it may be the reader of this book!

- **Fast tracking** – getting your product to the market before your competitors (while keeping your retiring employee motivated and interested until the process is formalised and all official documents signed).

- **Team roles** and relationships that are subject to change and need to be developed, defined and established (team building).

As a Human Resources specialist, you no doubt are no stranger to change and thrive on seeing positive results in changing environments.

To give any idea or concept the best chance of success, it is always useful to look at what other people in other companies and countries do. This is also known as best practice.

An article by Carol Hymowitz[13] informs us that with 10,000 baby boomers turning 65 each day, manufacturing, financial services and other companies are increasingly concerned about an exodus of their most experienced employees. Some are seeking ways to ensure that veterans pass along their knowledge to younger colleagues before they leave the workplace.

One solution is phased retirement. Employers offering this benefit allow older employees to work part time or on flexible schedules for several months or years before they choose to retire. Fourteen percent of U.S. companies are currently offering either a formal or informal phased retirement programme, up from 10 percent in 2012, according to the Society for Human Resource Management.

More companies need to do this if they want to preserve their best practices, innovations and customer relations. It's a choice many workers in their 60s welcome. Instead of ending long careers all at once, they want to stay engaged but in new ways.

Growing numbers of older employees also can't afford to stop working when they reach traditional retirement age and appreciate the chance to work part time. Fifty-nine percent of American households headed by people who are 65 and older currently have no retirement account assets, according to Federal Reserve data analysed by the National Institute on Retirement Security.

At First Horizon National in Memphis, employees can reduce their work schedules to 20 to 30 hours weekly if their duties can be performed in that amount of time and they're willing to mentor successors. They also must commit to staying on for one to three years. The extra cost of keeping these veterans on their staff is worth it, top executives at First Horizon National say, because they're helping to train a younger generation of workers and managers.

Steelcase, the office furniture maker, started offering phased retirement in 2012 when it realised it would soon face a tsunami of retiring Baby Boomers, especially in its IT department and manufacturing plants. Currently, about 800 employees or 15 percent of Steelcase's U.S. workforce, are eligible to retire based on years of service and age. So far, 47 have elected phased departures and more are expected to in coming years. Among them are Steelcase's most skilled electrician at the company's Grand Rapids, Mich., plant, who's 65 and now putting in 30 hours over four work days every week, instead of his former six-day-a-week schedule.

Phased retirement arrangements require adjustments on the part of both workers and their bosses. Managers must organise part-time work schedules which fit their work flows. Veterans have to get used to not always being the "go-to" workers when problems arise, and to accept that the younger people they're mentoring will inevitably make decisions and do work tasks differently from the way they do. As one older worker who's doing phased retirement at Steelcase said, "It's like being a parent letting go of a child and not resenting that."

But the adjustments are worth making. At a time when companies are competing for the best talent, employers can't afford to let their most experienced workers walk out the door the moment they celebrate their sixtieth or sixty-fifth birthdays.

Quick Tip

Use the functionality of your HRMS to plan your succession and to stay on top of time-sensitive events like your ERP.

By acting timeously and planning your ERP well, your organisation can ensure that top talent is trained, retained, and that they remain.

The work schedule of any modern-day Human Resources person is usually hectic, to say the least, and everything possible must be done to meet deadlines, plan manpower and ensure job match – to name but a few. To this end, equally important is that projects, like our ERP, are planned and executed in such a manner that sufficient time is allowed for inevitable delays. As our mutual friend and compatriot, Murphy states, "If anything can go wrong, it will – at the worst possible time!" Of course, we do not plan to succumb to such things as rotten luck. However, reality rules and life happens, so plan accordingly.

How does one allow "enough" time and what does this all mean?

According to Amanda Abella,[14] a business owner and head of (HR) department, you run into one of two issues. The first is procrastinating because you think you have more time than you actually do. The second is thinking projects will take less time than they actually do. The struggle is real, which is why business owners need to learn how to allow enough time on their calendar for projects. The first thing to realise is that there really is no right or wrong way to do this. However, there are some tips you can use to figure out what works for you. Here's how to allow enough time on your calendar for projects.

Learn from experience

Sometimes knowing how much time we need to put on our calendar for projects is a matter of experience. As time goes on and you have more experience running a business, you'll know how long projects actually take.

Just note that you'll totally screw this up in the beginning. That's okay because you're still learning your own rhythm. One week a project will take a couple of hours and the next week the same project will take five.

Use time-tracking to help you

One thing you can do to help you organise your calendar for projects is to track your time for a few weeks. Lots of invoicing services come with a time-tracking feature you can use. You can also do it the old-fashioned way with a timer. What you'll want to do is use the time-tracker for each project. Meaning, if you have two different projects, then track the time separately. Another option is to track your time based on similar types of projects. For example, how long does it take you to complete a series of blog posts?

Once you have a few weeks' worth of data, you can calculate the average time it takes you to complete certain projects. This gives you a starting point you can use to allow enough time on your calendar for projects. By the way, you can do this for meetings too. The good news is with meetings you have more control over the situation so you don't waste time.

Always give yourself a cushion

Despite our best efforts, it's safe to assume that projects will take us more time than we anticipated. Sometimes they take us less time, but even if that's the case you always want to give yourself a cushion for those times when you are delayed. For example, let's say your calculations tell you a particular task usually takes you three hours on average. You may want to allow an extra hour to be safe. So, with the example I gave earlier, I would allow three hours on my calendar for that weekly project. It's somewhere in the middle and it gives me some extra wiggle room.

Final thoughts

Learning how to allow enough time on your calendar for projects is a learning process. Don't stress about it too much as you'll get better at it with time. We are in the fortunate position of having so many examples of people who have experienced or currently still experience the same situation and potential frustrations; and on some rare occasions, embarrassment. Most people enjoy a good story and, after some digging around in my own library and the internet, I came across the following good story, which so nicely illustrates a very important aspect of allowing enough time to successfully complete whatever it is you are busy with.

Gertrude Boyle began life as a German Jew in the 1920s. Her family got away from the Nazis in the nick of time and moved to the west coast of the United States in 1939, when she was 13. Safe in her new country, Gertrude learned English, finished high school, and went on to college in Arizona, where she met her future husband.

Years later, at the age of 47, she was faced with another very difficult situation. Her husband died of a heart attack, leaving her alone with their two children and a small clothing store in dire straits. A housewife up to that point, Gertrude knew absolutely nothing about running a business. On top of that, her husband had just taken out a $150,000 loan, using their home as collateral. The next few years were turbulent. The store almost went belly-up on several occasions. But Gertrude kept at it, and eventually she grew the business into the publicly traded company known as Columbia Sportswear.

An interviewer spoke to Gertrude Boyle about her mindset, to try to gain some insight into what makes the difference between people who generally reach their goals and those who generally don't. The first thing noteworthy about her thinking: In her late forties, faced with a catastrophe, she didn't view her situation as particularly difficult. Having already lived through a major challenge as a young teenager, she knew the best thing to do was to avoid playing the victim, instead focusing her efforts on what she could do today and tomorrow. She also took the view that although she understood nothing about business, she could work at it and get the hang of it. *Success or failure had nothing to do with her self-image; they were just the outcome of a learning process.* When funds were short and banks came after her in the early years, she didn't take it as an indication that she was a loser. It simply meant that she had to learn a little more.

One may be tempted to ask, "So where does time management of projects feature in this story?" Well, the secret ingredient is *your attitude* towards the task, project or programme you are currently working on.

Psychologists such as Carol Dweck[15] tell us that people have two opposing attitudes toward any given goal:

- We may strive to achieve an outcome as a way of demonstrating current capacity. For example, we sometimes view getting ahead at work as a way of showing that we're smarter than other people. This attitude is said to be *performance-oriented*.

- On the other hand, we might set out to achieve a goal with the view that we can learn to "do what it takes". If we stumble a little on the way, it simply means that we haven't learned everything. And reaching the end says nothing about our capacity; it's just the result of steady work. This kind of thinking constitutes a *learning-oriented* attitude.

No matter what time-management tools you utilise to work for you, if you have a performance-oriented attitude, you'll shrink from the prospect of failure. That's because you interpret a bad outcome to mean that you actually don't possess the capacity you were trying to show off.

People with this mindset either give up when faced with obstacles, or they put things off. Studies show that the *number one cause of procrastination is that the person's ego is attached to the outcome*. Think of how many people do all the work toward a PhD, only to stop short of completing the dissertation. Have you ever wondered why PhD candidates quit at the point where they have to reveal the most about themselves?

The best results are always achieved when an event, project or programme is well planned, well timed and well executed; there is no other way. The same principles apply to your ERP – start at the right time, execute timeously and you will be rewarded with motivated and happy employees, and above all, you will retain your best talent.

1. Employee Lifecycle	2. Retirement Planning	3. Be Kind Practical, and Real	4. Begin Early Enough	5. Support is Vital	6. Prepare for the New Role	7. Welcome them to their New Role	8. The Final Goodbyes

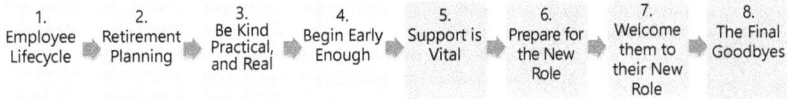

Summary of Chapter 4: Begin Early Enough

1. Treat the retiree's transition as a project, complete with a budget. HR people must ensure that a suitable budget is allocated so that the importance of this key labour force planning component is reinforced.

2. Assist the retiree in setting goals and aligning them to the organisational goals.

3. Make a diary entry, with regular follow-ups, as soon as possible – time waits for no-one. Share each step of the plan with the retiring employee.

Chapter 5

Support is Vital

Let me give you a hand...

> Your small support could accomplish a big dream.
> *Mohammad Rishad Sakhi*

DID YOU KNOW?
58% of South Africans expect to continue to work for pay after formal retirement and for the majority, this will be due to financial necessity rather than choice.[16]

Introduction

While sitting in my office in Johannesburg a couple of years ago, one of the company payroll ladies (who I will call Frances) working at a remote location, phoned me in a terrible state. What she told me about her personal problems and the decisions she faced, will stay with me for the rest of my life. This 28-year-old woman needed help and she needed it fast. I put the phone down and just knew, she needed support. She did not need money or any other material assistance – she needed support. After a couple of visits to a doctor and counselling psychologist, as well as the opportunity to resign with immediate effect without any limiting conditions, Frances left our employment and duly wrote me the most beautiful letter of appreciation. The golden thread throughout the two-page letter was "Thank you for your support." From a pragmatic perspective, the total cost of the support was about R2 000 – a negligible amount compared to the work she had done for the company and the value she added.

This true story is one of many, which clearly explains the importance of support in general. Exactly the same applies to all situations when, in this case, employees are facing dramatic change (preparing for retirement) and have to say goodbye to certain things that are near and dear to them.

So, handle...with...care!

Once an employee retires, they're likely to need something besides their hobbies to occupy their time. Unfortunately, many people enter their retirement years without determining what their next passion will be.

"You need a reason to get out of bed in the morning," says Tom Hegna,[17] a retirement planner, author and speaker based in Fountain Hills, Ariz. "Being in the workforce gives people a sense of belonging and importance. It is often their sense of power. They enjoy having people look to them for answers. It gives them a feeling of fulfilment. But once they leave the workforce, they often lose that." The loss of social interaction and the loss of the sense of belonging can be mitigated by supporting the retiring employee in planning for the last day at work, or in planning for the next exciting phase of their lives.

The Importance of Support

The first step in this next phase of the ERP is to decide on the best way to communicate the essence of the retiring employee's new role within the organisation. By now, the planning has been done, a timeframe agreed upon, heads of departments have been notified and a contract has been signed between the company and the retiring employee, so there is no reason why not to communicate this information to the relevant people within the enterprise. By "relevant people" it is understood that all people who came into contact with the retiring employee, should be communicated with. One can rather over-communicate than under-communicate; it is very easy to be trapped into a sense of "everybody knows" and thereby torpedo a great plan and leave the retiring employee with a less-than-pleasant feeling – one does not want that to happen at all.

The second step is to acknowledge the countdown milestones to the "new beginnings" of the retiring employee. There are various methods which one can use this, for example, memoranda, company/ department newsletters, general email or at monthly meetings. By acknowledging and announcing the countdown milestones, you will be:

- Keeping the employees' colleagues informed.

- Creating a sense of excitement.

- Building the employee's confidence and positively influencing their sense of belonging.

This kind of support goes a long way in ensuring you retain and nurture the very people who could be responsible for retaining and nurturing your other talented people. (I prefer the expression "talented people" to just "talent" – it is more personal). Other people to bear in mind, when acknowledging and sharing countdown milestones, are any other organisational stakeholders like customers and suppliers – if the retiring employee has interacted with any of these people during their tenure at the company.

There are all sorts of support and care groups for people going through transitions, says Robert Laura[18]. There are programmes for those who are struggling with the loss of a loved one, addiction, divorce, anger and boundaries, but there aren't any groups for people struggling with retirement. At least not yet, and if there are, they are few and far between.

There's a void in the area for a couple of important reasons. The first has to do with how the general public perceives retirement. Unlike undesirable things such as divorce, anger, widowhood, or alcohol abuse, retirement is supposed to be a good thing that people look forward to and make the most of. After all, you spend most of your working life looking forward to this magic time of no bosses, little stress and lots of free time. People assume it's this glorious stage where new time and freedoms unleash opportunities to spend more time with a spouse, children, and grandchildren, rekindle old passions and hobbies, and explore new places, customs, and cultures as they travel the globe.

Laura goes on to explain that it could feel much, much different...

- What if you don't fit in or feel comfortable in retirement?
- What if you miss work, don't get along with your spouse?
- What if you get sick of chasing your kids across the country as they move from place to place for new jobs?
- What if you're bored, don't feel compelled to get out of bed every day, and you are gaining weight?

That's not supposed to be how retirement looks and feels! You're supposed to be happy, engaged and fulfilled. You should be grateful for getting to this point in your life, and people should appreciate your knowledge and skills instead of just brushing you off or downplaying your credentials and value. It can be a confusing time with no immediate relief in sight.

The second issue is, who's going to admit it? Let's face it, many people who seek out support for anger management or addiction have to go because they are court-ordered. Court-ordered attendance may also come up in divorce cases if custody or other factors are involved. And let's not forget that a good portion of new widows/widowers are hesitant to join a grief group as they feel their situation is different or that their needs may not be met or understood by the group. And, as in so many situations in life, just at the very time one needs support, hoards of people aren't waiting in the wings to support and guide.

After all, who wants to be vulnerable and the poster child for not being able to replace their work identity, fill their time, grow closer to family and friends, or stay current and relevant? It's a double-edged sword because it's very common to have feelings like this about life in retirement, but until you're there, it's hard to comprehend or empathise with. One should also take note of the fact that the concept of traditional retirement is fatally flawed. In fact, it's founded on half-truths and bad assumptions. That's why so many people are hell bent on finding another way to define or describe it. The good news is that there's not something wrong with you, there's something wrong with how we have all been programmed to think about and prepare for retirement. We've been brainwashed with this foolish, Utopian-type belief system where life finally comes together and flows with little energy or effort. But nothing could be further from the truth. A successful life in retirement isn't one without problems but rather one where you learn to overcome them.

Quick Tip

Consider including the ERP progress in the HR section of the exco and/or board report. And do not accept any excuse that it is just an "HR" issue – it should be part of the organisational strategy!

Retirement takes work! People need new skills, mindsets, scheduled activities and more. But because people walk into it with old and outdated ideas about it, they can quickly find themselves lost or feeling out of sorts. People need to be reprogrammed (read supported) to go into retirement with more than just a written financial plan. They need a concrete, written plan for what everyday life will look like and feel like. They need to work with a trained and experienced retirement coach to truly understand what it takes to make a successful transition, including hurdles that can set them back as well as opportunities they need to take advantage of right away. There's no benefit to walking into retirement and wasting the first, and some of the best years, trying to figure it out, when there are professionals and a proven process for turning this time into what you want it to be rather than hoping and praying it will take care of itself. If your company prides itself that "our people are our most important asset" it should reflect in mission, strategy and budget allocation. If not, now may be the best time to do so.

In order to better understand the actual responsibility that a CHRO and their team have towards preparing employees for retirement, it may be useful to briefly discuss the big role leadership plays in transitioning the HR department and/or the company from good (i.e. mediocre) to great (best in class). And what better guidelines to use that those shared with the world by Jim Collins in his world best-selling book, *From Good to Great*.[19]

The following summary will enable the open-minded and motivated amongst us to better deal with this great transition:

Why the Quest for Good to Great?

Good to Great answers the search for enduring excellence. It is not just a business problem; it's a human problem. The principles within this book can be applied to other organisations, not just business enterprises. Good schools can learn to become great schools. Good government agencies can learn to be great government agencies.

"Level 5 Leadership"

Level 5 leaders channel their ego needs away from themselves and into the larger goal of building a great company. Their ambition is first and foremost for the institution/organisation, not themselves.

Level 1: Highly Capable Individual
- Makes productive contributions through talent, knowledge, skills, and good work habits.

Level 2: Contributing Team Member
- Contributes individual capabilities to the group objective, works well in a group setting.

Level 3: Competent Manager
- Organises people and resources towards efficient and effective pursuit of objectives.

Level 4: Effective Leader
- Catalyst, vigorous pursuit of vision, stimulates higher performance standards.

Level 5: Executive
- Builds enduring greatness through a paradoxical blend of personal humility and professional will.

David Maxwell of Fannie Mae, Darwin Smith of Kimberly-Clark, and Colman Mockler of Gillette exemplify a key trait of Level 5 leaders: ambition for the company and concern for its success rather than one's own personal fortune. They think not in terms of "I" but "We".

**Level 5 = Humility + Professional Will +
Modesty + Resolve + Determination**

Good to great leaders never wanted to be larger-than-life icons or heroes. They were ordinary people quietly working and producing extraordinary results.

Good to Great Level 5 leaders:

- Are results-oriented.

- Possess inspired standards. They do not tolerate mediocrity.

- Never allow nepotism or seniority. They will fire non-performing family members and friends.

- Are insiders. They have worked many years inside the company or are from the family that owns the company. They are not saviours hired in from the outside.

- Are diligent. They are not show horses but plough horses.

- Choose good successors because of their concern for the future of the company. They want to see it endure for generations.

- Possess determination. Darwin Smith sold the paper mills of Kimberly-Clark to focus on consumer products. Everyone else was saying it was a bad move, but they were wrong. Cork Walgreen decided to get out of the food business and into the more lucrative business of convenience drugstores.

The Window and the Mirror

Level 5 leaders give credit to outside factors when things go well (looking out the window), and take full responsibility when things go poorly (looking at the mirror). The comparison companies' leaders blame outside factors when things go poorly, and credit the company's successes to themselves.

Two Sides of Level 5 Leaders

Professional Will and Personal Humility

- Creates superb results.
- A catalyst in good to great transition.
- Modest. Shuns public adulation. Never boastful.
- Unwavering resolve. Does whatever it takes to produce long-term results.
- Acts with quiet, calm determination. Relies on inspired standards, not charisma, to motivate.
- Sets the standard for building an enduring company. Settles for nothing less.
- Channels ambition into the company not the self. Sets up successors for success in the next generation.

How does one find potential Level 5 leaders?

1. Look for situations where extraordinary results exist yet no individual steps forth to claim the credit.
2. Level 5 leaders practise self-reflection, had good parents, a significant life experience, a level 5 boss, or a great mentor.

Key points:

1. Every good to great company had Level 5 leadership during pivotal transition years.

2. Level 5 leaders set up their successors for even greater success in the future, while egocentric Level 4 leaders often set up their successors for failure.

3. Level 5 leaders display a compelling modesty, are self-effacing and understated. In contrast, two thirds of the comparison companies had leaders with gargantuan personal egos that contributed to the demise or continued mediocrity of the company.

4. Level 5 leaders are fanatically driven, infected with an incurable need to produce sustained results. They are resolved to do whatever it takes to make the company great, no matter how big or hard the decisions.

5. One of the most damaging trends in recent history is the tendency (especially of boards of directors) to select dazzling, celebrity leaders and to de-select potential Level 5 leaders.

6. Potential Level 5 leaders exist all around us, we just have to know what to look for.

7. The third and final step is to arrange a special socio-work event to say goodbye to the "old" employee and to welcome the "new" employee.

TIME TO PARTY!!

Now is the time to create the excitement for the upcoming goodbyes to old roles and hello's to new and exciting roles! To ensure that the buzz is kept alive, it is a good idea to start building the hype by arranging a really fun and enjoyable party event. Before naysayers roll the ever-popular "we have no budget for this type of nonsense" rock of obstruction into your path, let us be reminded that we are talking about our most important asset... lest we forget!

| 1. Employee Lifecycle | 2. Retirement Planning | 3. Be Kind Practical, and Real | 4. Begin Early Enough | 5. Support is Vital | 6. Prepare for the New Role | 7. Welcome them to their New Role | 8. The Final Goodbyes |

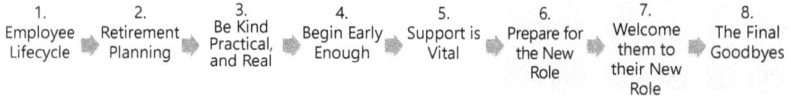

Summary of Chapter 5: Support is Vital

1. Be kind and structured.

2. Think carefully about the actual new role as well as how to communicate it.

3. Apply Level 5 Leadership principles.

4. Take total ownership. Share each step of the plan with the retiring employee.

Chapter 6

Prepare for the New Role

New Things, Fun Things

> Change can be frightening, and the temptation is often to resist it. But change almost always provides opportunities – to learn new things, to rethink tired processes, and to improve the way we work.
> *Klaus Schwab*

> **DID YOU KNOW?**
> *People don't resist change; they resist being changed.*
> *(Peter Senge)*

Introduction

This saying sums up very nicely the feelings our retiring employee will most probably experience, sooner or later. Different people respond differently to change; however, one fact does always remain, change requires a different way of seeing things, a different perspective, a transformation. In my professional HR career, I have found that by preparing people for new roles or situations, the end result is always much better than without any preparation. In my previous book, *Transformation in 28 Days*,[20] one chapter is dedicated to a most useful and practical method of adapting to change and of making a transformational leap in a manner that is non-threatening and successful.

Life has a way of sneaking up on one. One moment you're a carefree kid and the next, well, you've become part of your environment, shaped by the pressures of reality. Those hopes and dreams of youth have all but faded from memory, leaving the slightest trace of regret.

Change tends to be a good thing and we often discover new ways to experience satisfaction no matter the circumstances. But wouldn't it be great if there were a way to reach back in time and reclaim the excitement of your younger years? What if you could slow time's relentless march and savour each passing moment? Perhaps you'd spend that time rebuilding the hope and compassion of an earlier time, before the hassles and worry of adulthood.

The 6 Swedberg Keys to Personal Transformation

This section should be made available to retiring employees as a self-help guide to assist them in making the transition easier:

👣 Step 1: Craft Your Vision

You are a conscious being trapped in a physical body. In order to create real and lasting change on the outside, you need to organise your internal world. This begins with a simple question: **what do you want?**

There is no shame in not knowing immediately. In fact, I ask myself this question almost every day and the answer seems to change constantly depending on my mood, environment, and recent experiences. However, over time, you can identify a theme and as you compare those similar answers you will eventually discover a purpose.

By 'purpose' I mean a driving desire to change the world in a specific way. This generally falls into one of two categories . . .

- **Correction:** you have experienced a grievous pain in the past and are now driven to protect others from the same fate.
- **Contribution:** you have enjoyed a wonderful experience in the past and desire to share that same pleasure with the world.

The best way to discover what you want is to continually ask yourself questions. Rely on your new friends: ask what, why, how, when, where, and who. They will guide you through this process and eventually bring you to your true identity. After all, you were born to change the world, so stop saying "I can't" and have a little faith!

Step 2: Increase Your Knowledge

Creating a vision for improving the world is just the first step. Next you're going to need to develop the wisdom and skill to make your dreams come true. This begins with learning.

Let's face it, most of us have been moulded by the expectations of our peer group and work environment. We probably know a little bit too much about the NFL and Facebook, but our knowledge of influence and change is pitifully small.

This step requires some courage. It's going to take time and humility to submit to the rigours of self-education. You'll need to read books, browse blog posts, dig through Wikipedia, and maybe even watch a documentary or two.

The good news is that once you get started, you'll discover a burning passion that drives you forward. This is what you've always wanted and even if you can't have it today, at least you are one step closer to realising your destiny.

Step 3: Be Open to Feedback

The real trick is to avoid overconfidence. I'd be lying if I told you I've never made this mistake or that you will somehow avoid it. However, you can minimise the risk of premature action if you remain humble and are willing to adapt.

Feedback is essential for progress. It is nature's way of letting us know when to turn and how fast to move. I'm not just talking about what Uncle Bob decides to share with you over the holidays. I'm saying you need to look at the results of your actions and ask: 'Is what I'm doing working?'

Track your progress. Measure something tangible. Find a way to wrap your head around the process. Otherwise, you'll charge blindly into walls forever. From personal experience, I can assure you that is both a painful and extremely slow way to proceed.

👣 Step 4: Embrace the Culture

Once you gain knowledge of your chosen path and get a little experience walking that road, you might want to consider finding other warriors on a similar journey. The world is an awfully big place, and recently it's all been crammed into the space of your computer screen.

Take advantage of this amazing resource to find like-minded people. Share your vision, or at least your current step, and don't be afraid to ask for help. Chances are you'll make some friends and maybe even discover a mentor or two.

The best part about getting involved in an established culture, whether it's a local group of people or an online platform like a blog, is the positive reinforcement you'll receive. Psychologists say that we are the aggregate of the five people we spend the most time with. As you change your peer group, you'll also change your influences. You've essentially created your own environment and taken control of your personal evolution. Say hello to natural, effortless personal transformation!

👣 Step 5: Track Your Progress

Now that you're equipped with the basic tools of self-growth, it's time to see results. Break down your vision into milestones, goals, and steps.

Set small objectives that are easy to accomplish. Not only will this help you focus on the next and most important move, but it will reward you with a constant sense of accomplishment. We all know that progress equals excitement, so make sure to create a plan that keeps you energised and motivated to keep working!

👣 Step 6: Keep Things in Perspective

You've become a true warrior. The world is in your hands and even though your training may span years, you've managed to recapture your dreams and turn them into something real and doable.

Sadly, most people stop here. I've done it too. We forget that life isn't about accomplishment or glory. It's about experience, about enjoying every moment in the most fulfilling way. No result or achievement can ever make up for a life wasted in work and worry.

Remember, life is a journey. It's important to choose a worthwhile destination and take those first steps, but after that, sit back, relax, and enjoy the ride. After all, it's all you get. Make it count

As this exciting journey gets closer to the next best thing for employer and employee, it is important that the matter of change is dealt with and used. Let us not forget that the change faced by someone retiring after a full, busy and happy life is no small thing. It is massive!

Change... written about so much, spoken about even more and continuously experienced, one way or the other. According to the Collins English Dictionary, change is defined as *"to make or become different, to replace with or exchange for another"*. Wikipedia gives a bit more clarity by defining change as *"a difference in a state of affairs at different points in time, activities that improve awareness and identity, an alteration in the social order of a society (or person.)"*.

One thing is very clear and that is that change is an uncertain and complex phenomenon which all people face, sooner or later. Two people who understand change very well and have done extensive amounts of research about change are Dr John Kotter and Elizabeth Kübler-Ross. Where Dr Kotter (Kotter's Eight Steps of Change)[21] focuses more on organisational change, Elizabeth Kübler-Ross (Kübler-Ross Change Curve) focuses more on personal or individual change. For the purposes of this guide, the Kübler-Ross Change Curve[22] is most appropriate and is described in some detail below.

The Change Curve

The Change Curve is based on a model originally developed in the 1960s by Elisabeth Kübler-Ross to explain the grieving process. Since then it has been widely utilised as a method of helping people understand their reactions to significant change or upheaval. Kübler-Ross proposed that a terminally ill patient would progress through five stages of grief when informed of their illness. She further proposed that this model could be applied to any dramatic life-changing situation and, by the 1980s, the Change Curve was a firm fixture in change management circles. The curve, and its associated emotions, can be used to predict how performance is likely to be affected by the announcement and subsequent implementation of a significant change. The original five stages of grief – denial, anger, bargaining, depression and acceptance – have adapted over the years. There are numerous versions of the curve in existence. However, the majority of them are consistent in their use of the following basic emotions, which are often grouped into three distinct transitional stages.

Quick Tip

*Do a dipstick test on your own readiness for change and be very honest with yourself;
are you a change agent or a true transformer?
You should be a transformer!*

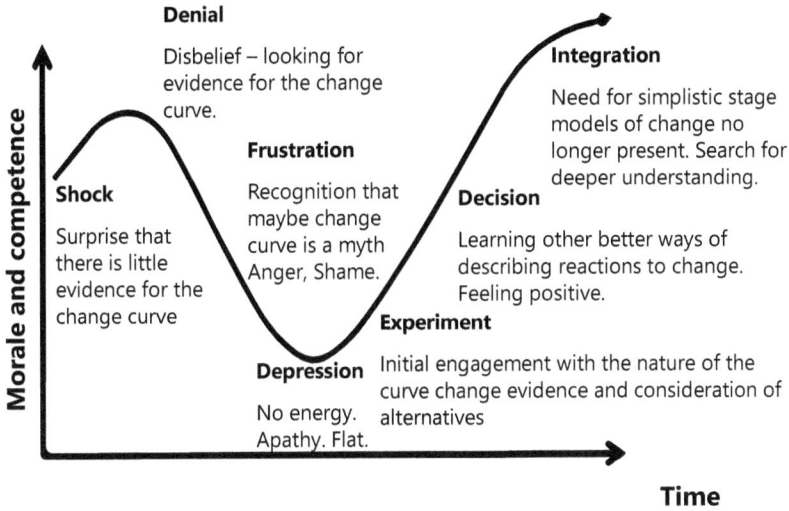

The change curve diagram showing Morale and competence on the vertical axis and Time on the horizontal axis:

Denial
Disbelief – looking for evidence for the change curve.

Shock
Surprise that there is little evidence for the change curve

Frustration
Recognition that maybe change curve is a myth Anger, Shame.

Depression
No energy. Apathy. Flat.

Experiment
Initial engagement with the nature of the curve change evidence and consideration of alternatives

Decision
Learning other better ways of describing reactions to change. Feeling positive.

Integration
Need for simplistic stage models of change no longer present. Search for deeper understanding.

Figure 1: The Kübler-Ross change curve[23]

Stage 1 – Shock and denial

The first reaction to change is usually shock. This initial shock, while frequently short lived, can result in a temporary slowdown and loss of productivity. Performance tends to dip sharply, individuals who are normally clear and decisive seek more guidance and reassurance, and agreed deadlines can be missed.

The shock is often due to:

- lack of information;
- fear of the unknown; and
- fear of looking stupid or doing something wrong.

After the initial shock has passed, it is common for individuals to experience denial. At this point focus tends to remain in the past. There's likely to be a feeling that as everything was OK as it was, why does there need to be a change?

Common feelings include:

- being comfortable with the status quo;
- feeling threatened; and
- fear of failure.

Individuals who have not previously experienced major change can be particularly affected by this first stage. It is common for people to convince themselves that the change isn't actually going to happen, or if it does, that it won't affect them. Performance often returns to the levels seen before the dip experienced during the initial shock of the change. People carry on as they always have and may deny having received communication about the changes, and may well make excuses to avoid taking part in forward planning. At this stage, communication is key. Reiterating what the actual change is, the effects it may have, and providing as much reassurance as possible, will all help to support individuals experiencing these feelings.

Stage 2 – Anger and depression

After the feelings of shock and denial, anger is often the next stage. A scapegoat, in the shape of an organisation, group or individual, is commonly found. Focusing the blame on someone or something allows a continuation of the denial by providing another focus for the fears and anxieties the potential impact is causing.

Common feelings include:

- suspicion;
- scepticism; and
- frustration.

The lowest point of the curve comes when the anger begins to wear off and the realisation that the change is genuine hits. It is common for morale to be low, and for self-doubt and anxiety levels to peak.

Feelings during this stage can be hard to express, and depression is possible as the impact of what has been lost is acknowledged.
This period can be associated with:

- apathy;

- isolation; and

- remoteness.

At this point performance is at its lowest. There is a tendency to fixate on small issues or problems, often to the detriment of day-to-day tasks. Individuals may continue to perform tasks in the same way as before, even if this is no longer appropriate behaviour. People will be reassured by the knowledge that others are experiencing the same feelings. Providing managers, teams and individuals with information about the Change Curve underlines that the emotions are usual and shared, and this can help to develop a more stable platform from which to move into the final stage.

Stage 3 – Acceptance and integration

After the darker emotions of the second stage, a more optimistic and enthusiastic mood begins to emerge. Individuals accept that change is inevitable, and begin to work with the changes rather than against them.

Now come thoughts of:

- exciting new opportunities;

- relief that the change has been survived; and

- impatience for the change to be complete.

The final steps involve integration. The focus is firmly on the future and there is a sense that real progress can now be made. By the time everyone reaches this stage, the changed situation has firmly replaced the original and becomes the new reality.

The primary feelings now include:

- acceptance;
- hope; and
- trust.

During the early part of this stage, energy and productivity remain low, but slowly begin to show signs of recovery. Everyone will have lots of questions and be curious about possibilities and opportunities. Normal topics of conversation resume, and a wry humour is often used when referring to behaviour earlier in the process.

Individuals will respond well to being given specific tasks or responsibilities, however communication remains key. Regular progress reports and praise help to cement the more buoyant mood. It is not uncommon for there to be a return to an earlier stage if the level of support suddenly drops.

Individual reactions

Each person reacts individually to change, and not all will experience every phase. Some people may spend a lot of time in stages 1 and 2, whilst others who are more accustomed to change may move fairly swiftly into stage 3. Although it is generally acknowledged that moving from stage 1 through stage 2 and finally to stage 3 is most common, there is no right or wrong sequence. Several people going through the same change at the same time are likely to travel at their own speed, and will reach each stage at different times.

Summary

The Change Curve is a very useful tool when managing individual or team change. Knowing where an individual is on the curve will help when deciding on how and when to communicate information, what level of support someone requires, and when best to implement final changes. Furnishing individuals with the knowledge that others understand and experience similar emotions is the best way to return, with as little pain as possible, to optimal performance.

The good news, dear reader, is that you do not have to waste any time in experimenting or going through what-if scenarios; the guidelines you are given above, if used correctly and by allowing enough time, will be successful. They have been researched, tried and tested over and over again.

The closer one gets to the actual time of changeover to the new role, the more the need to communicate regularly and timeously – one does not want the retiring employee to feel in the least uncertain or to get the feeling that this new chapter of their lives is not being properly executed.

Training for the new role

With the relevant tools now firmly in their toolbox, retiree and employer can now agree on the training required for the new role. We should bear in mind that although the retiree has a load of experience and knowledge in a range of positions, this new role will, most probably, be different from anything else they have done until that point of their lives. Therefore, deciding which supporting training to attend is very important. What follows next is a short (and by no means conclusive) list of potential roles and relevant training.

Possible new roles for the retiring employee:

1. Coach
2. Mentor
3. Trainer
4. Training Material Developer
5. Policy Document Editor
6. Office Support Manager
7. Technical Problem Solver
8. Key Account Manager

9. Sales Support (for instance to help with demonstrations and technical expertise)

10. Employee Relations Officer

11. Security Specialist

There are endless opportunities for this person to fulfil and the specific role will depend on the type of sector, industry and company. A thorough conversation between HR, retiree and the head of Learning and Development, should be held as soon as possible to agree on the next steps of ensuring that the retiree has a clear idea of what is expected of them and what role the various stakeholders are to play. The outcome of this meeting is to be recorded in an action plan with dates which are reconcilable with the actual retirement date.

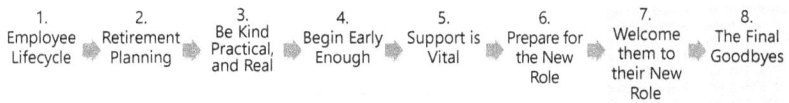

1. Employee Lifecycle	2. Retirement Planning	3. Be Kind Practical, and Real	4. Begin Early Enough	5. Support is Vital	6. Prepare for the New Role	7. Welcome them to their New Role	8. The Final Goodbyes

Summary of Chapter 6: Prepare for the New Role

1. It is important that employer and retiree are prepared for the imminent change.

2. Share The 6 Swedberg Keys to Personal Transformation as well as the Kübler-Ross Model. These two tools will help prepare them for their training and also their new role.

3. Schedule a meeting between HR, L&D and the retiree to agree on the training expectations and to sign off an action plan.

4. Ensure that training and assignments are completed by the relevant dates to ensure a seamless transition from one role to the next.

5. Keep the retiree thoroughly in the loop at all times – things can get a bit crazy and it is easy to forget.

Chapter 7

Welcome Them to Their New Role

To welcome is to respect.

> When we are generous in welcoming people and sharing something with them – some food, a place in our homes, our time – not only do we no longer remain poor: we are enriched. I am well aware that when someone needing food knocks at your door, you always find a way of sharing food; as the proverb says, one can always 'add more water to the beans'! Is it possible to add more water to the beans?... Always?...
> And you do so with love, demonstrating that true riches consist not in materials things, but in the heart!
> *Pope Francis*

> **DID YOU KNOW?**
> *Organisations that invest in a strong candidate improve the quality of their new hires by 70 percent.*[24]

Introduction

One of the best experiences ever, I think, is being welcomed to an event, place, new job or any new situation. That feeling of being known, expected, valued and made to feel part of the new happenings immediately, is something which, unfortunately, is lacking in businesses all over the globe. In spite of beautiful buzz words, fads and top-of-the-range onboarding plans, programmes, endeavours and high-definition photos, splashed all over bright and shiny corporate brochures, there are still too many people who have had terrible "first days" at a new job. If the tone of the previous two sentences sounds a bit harsh, well, it is meant to be!

Too many companies employ managers (not leaders, because a leader does what is right) who have very little respect for others and when it comes to welcoming new employees or newly promoted or newly transferred employees, they are nowhere to be seen. It is necessary to drive this point home with a bit of vigour and passion so that when we proceed with the welcoming of the retiree to their new role, this person can glide into their new role and add value by knowing they are valued and that this has been demonstrated by a solid "Welcome!"

Now while it may seem to be common knowledge to the HR people, most of the enterprise's employees will not have enough information about the retiree's new role. It is, therefore, critical that information is shared in a correct, timeous and accurate manner and by following these seven principles[25] of communication, one can make the message more effective:

Principles of Communication

⚖ 1. Principle of Clarity

The idea or message to be communicated should be clearly spelt out. It should be worded in such a way that the receiver understands the same thing that the sender wants to convey. There should be no ambiguity in the message. It should be kept in mind that the words do not speak themselves but the speaker gives them meaning. A clear message will evoke the same response from the other party. It is also essential that the receiver is conversant with the language, inherent assumptions, and the mechanics of communication.

⚖ 2. Principle of Attention

In order to make communication effective, the receiver's attention should be drawn towards the message. People are different in behaviour, attention, emotions, etc. so they may respond in different ways to the message. Subordinates should act similarly as per the contents of the message. The acts of a superior also draw the attention of subordinates and they may follow what they observe.

For example, if a superior is very punctual in coming to the office then subordinates will also develop such habits. It is said that 'actions speak louder than words'.

⚖ 3. Principle of Feedback

The principle of feedback is very important to make the communication effective. There should be feedback information from the recipient that will indicate whether he or she has understood the message in the same sense in which the sender meant it.

⚖ 4. Principle of Informality

Formal communication is generally used for transmitting messages and other information. Sometimes formal communication may not achieve the desired results; informal communication may prove effective in such situations. Management should use informal communication for assessing the reaction of employees towards various policies. Senior management may informally convey certain decisions to the employees for getting their feedback. So this principle states that informal communication is as important as formal communication.

⚖ 5. Principle of Consistency

This principle states that communication should always be consistent with the policies, plans, programmes and objectives of the organisation and not in conflict with them. If the messages and communications are in conflict with the policies and programmes then there will be confusion in the minds of subordinates and they may not implement them properly. Such a situation will be detrimental to the interests of the organisation.

⚖ 6. Principle of Timeliness

This principle states that communication should be done at the proper time so that it helps in implementing plans. Any delay in communication may not serve any purpose; rather, decisions become of historical importance only.

⚖️ 7. Principle of Adequacy

The information communicated should be adequate and complete in all respects. Inadequate information may delay action and create confusion. Inadequate information also affects the efficiency of the receiver. So, adequate information is essential for taking proper decisions and making action plans.

Content of Communication

With some sound preparation about the retiree's imminent role and the communication thereof now behind us, we can focus on the content of the communication. Please note that the mode or medium of communication is not dealt with in this book; the preferred method/s of communication are so varied and particular to an organisation, that the assumption is made that the most suitable medium of communication will be used. If you do not have a company template or policy guideline available to you, an example is provided below.

Let us work with the following scenario: After qualifying as a junior manager, Max Smith joined the Great Service Company when he was 22 years old. He worked in various departments throughout his 43-year career with the company, facing extreme uncertainty and high stress levels when the company went through a tough time and some of his colleagues were retrenched. During an extremely tumultuous time, when the Great Service Company merged with another company, Max was tempted to leave, but pushed on and remained a loyal, hardworking employee.

About two years before his impending retirement, the Chief Human Resources Officer invited Max for an informal discussion to determine what his retirement and post-retirement plans were. The two of them agreed that Max would retire at the prescribed age of 65 years and then he would start his new career, with his existing employer, as trainer-coach to conduct onboarding, orientation and introductory training for new employees as well as newly promoted employees who were dealing with uncertainty and stress related to their new position. Max was prepared to work for an additional two years in his new capacity and would gradually scale down in his current job so as to prepare for his new role. It seemed like a perfect match from which both the company and Max could benefit tremendously. Within a couple of weeks an agreement was finalised and the Chief Human Resources Officer could notify Max's colleagues.

> **Quick Tip**
>
> *Ensure that you are very comfortable with writing any and all letters. Ask a friend or acquaintance who is good at letter writing to mentor you. Writing great letters goes a long way in strengthening your own skill set and credibility.*

Here is the CHRO's letter...

Dear Colleagues

MAX SMITH: RETIREMENT AND SUBSEQUENT NEW ROLE.

It is with more joy than sadness that we hereby notify you of the impending retirement of Mr. Max Smith, Human Resources Manager. Most of you have either worked for or alongside Max for the past 43 years and have learned that Max is a one-of-a-kind person who is not afraid to reach out and go further; you may recall his standing quote," So, what now, Captain?" Whenever a job or project was nearing completion, or sometimes just for fun's sake he would repeat his motto.

In line with our company's Employee Retirement Plan, negotiations started a while ago and we are very happy to announce that with effect from today, in 3 months, we will be having a party celebrating Max's retirement and his appointment as Group Employee Mentor!

We have managed to retain Max's skills, knowledge and great attitude for an additional 24 months, during which time he will take care of assisting promoted employees, new employees and anyone in need of some mentoring. He will also be gradually decreasing his time spent at work so that by the time he stops working, he will have adjusted to his new role of official retiree.

Closer the time, more details about his role and reporting lines will be shared – in the meantime, feel free to chat to Max about the process of preparing for retirement and how it benefits both employee and employer.

Kind Regards
CHRO

Style, length and company jargon will dictate the optimal wording for your particular enterprise. However, feel free to use this letter as a guide.

Now that the transition from employee to retiree has been communicated, one can expect that a fair amount of discussions and conversations will take place – this is a good thing. In the bigger scheme of things, a key characteristic of future-fit organisations is that they provide adequate platforms for conversation, even about contentious matters. The business leaders who know this, understand the following extract from *Developing Leaders*:[26]

> **"Why simple conversations are difficult to have**
> *Our research shows that three key factors co-conspire to make simple conversation difficult to do in today's business environment:*
>
> *First – time and place. With every promotion things seem to get busier and busier. As a result workplace conversations are increasingly about informing people, relaying decisions, talking through the 'to do' list of action points. To make matters worse it is difficult to find a place to have a conversation. With fewer private offices, workstations where everyone can overhear and meeting*

rooms fully booked for client meetings, informal chats are often relegated to the crowded Starbucks around the corner.

Secondly, technology has altered the way we communicate – less face-to-face, more texts, more e-mails. Without noticing we have become conditioned to a tsunami of electronic exchanges, which come ever faster, are ever shorter and ever more task-focused.

Lastly – the cult of the entertainer. Being a good communicator is no longer good enough. Bosses at all levels must now have the golden combination of being a rescuing super hero and engaging entertainer. Even professors at top business schools have become slick raconteurs and clever comedians endlessly presenting us with images of the iconic Jobs, the visionary Mandela or the audacious Branson."

One of my most rewarding experiences about welcoming a retiring employee to their new role is the story of Peter. Peter was an experienced scaffolding erector and worked for the same company as I did for many, many years. As is the situation with so many people who approach retirement age, Peter was worried, very worried. During one of our informal chats, he alluded to the fact that he will get "old and sick" if he has to retire at the age of 65. Now, I must add that Peter was an extremely fit and youthful 62-year-old with an amazing zest for life. To him, retirement meant the end of life as he knew it and he was not a happy fellow when his thoughts consumed him; he actually started to stress more and more about the matter.

Fast forward to Peter's 63rd birthday. I congratulated him and almost in passing asked if he would like to continue working after his 65th birthday. Well, what an overwhelming response from Peter! He was ecstatic and could not thank me enough for this amazing ray of hope in his dark mind. And so it happened that Peter turned 65, and he stayed on as scaffold erector trainer and administrator for a further three years. During the party to celebrate his leaving and "arriving" he had an opportunity to speak and he had us all in stitches when he bestowed the title of "doctor" on me, because "this man gave me a new heart!"

The story is precious, not because of an instant doctorate, but because the new lease on life, by preparing an employee for retirement, has given a real person, real hope and satisfaction.

The Role of Emotional Intelligence

As we gradually approach the end of this chapter, it is important to consider the role of emotional intelligence when preparing employees for retirement. For clarification and purposes of this book, emotional intelligence was described formally by Salovey and Mayer.[27] They defined it as 'the ability to monitor one's own and others' feelings and emotions, to discriminate among them and to use this information to guide one's thinking and actions'.

Daniel Goleman[28] defines emotional intelligence (EI) as the ability to:

- Recognise, understand and manage our own emotions.
- Recognise, understand and influence the emotions of others.

In practical terms, this means being aware that emotions can drive our behaviour and impact people (positively and negatively), and learning how to manage those emotions – both our own and others' – especially when we are under pressure. Just about as dangerous as making assumptions is the danger of considering retirement a transactional event which all people must go through. The emotional impact on an individual who has been working for about 40 years and is then to commence the next chapter of their lives by not being needed, should not be underestimated. Far too many times I have heard managers say that it is time for this or that person to "be retired, so that we can get in some young blood". This is an inexcusable attitude and one which cannot be tolerated in any organisation wishing to attract and retain top talent.

The best thing that HR people and line managers alike can do, to emotionally support a retiring employee, is the following:

- Commence discussions early enough.

- Be available to have a conversation with the person.

- Consider the person behind the title or role.

- Refrain from thinking or commenting about retirement as a necessary HR transaction.

Research indicates that overall emotional intelligence has promise as a predictor of various life outcomes, including mental and physical health.[29] Mental and physical health was included with various other characteristics in the "other performance" category. It is therefore most important that we address the emotional needs of the retiring employee so as to ensure that the company retains talent, together with health and happiness.

True and Legitimate Transformation

Last but not least, dear HR professional, are you ready and completely confident that you are on the right track and that you have undergone a certain amount of inner transformation as well? The following page or two will give you food for thought that may just spark a thought or trigger a behaviour that could stand you in good stead.

To craft a fitting conclusion to this phase and to set the scene for the next phase of your endeavours, it is important to understand the concept of legitimacy. True and legitimate transformation are two crucial concepts which should be woven into any transformation.

Being true to oneself and truthful, are principal values every person, who is serious about how they live their lives and conduct themselves, should possess and live unambiguously – no debate! It is up to each and every individual who embarks on any type of transformation, to clarify this for themselves and be at peace with it. Without it, no one should even consider embarking on a journey transformation – go for dinner, attend a sports match or chill instead!

This brings us to "legitimacy"... What exactly is this thing called legitimacy? A few different perspectives on the meaning of legitimacy will clarify it to a large extent; let's take a look:

In political science, legitimacy is the right and acceptance of an authority, usually a governing law or a régime.
In moral philosophy, the term "legitimacy" is often positively interpreted as the normative status conferred by a governed people upon their governors' institutions, offices, and actions, based upon the belief that their government's actions are appropriate uses of power by a legally constituted government.

Legitimacy is "a value whereby something or someone is recognised and accepted as right and proper".

Another perspective is to look at what "legitimate"means: Being exactly as purposed: neither spurious nor false <a legitimate grievance> <a legitimate practitioner>.

Taking all of the above and one's own context into account, the core of the matter is that your desire or decision to transform must be what you want! It must not be for the sake of a company, job, spouse, children, financial gain, spiritual elevation or any other external reason. You must want to because it is what you desire, what you need, or by not transforming you feel anxious. I think you get the point.

As with any action in life, there is always a risk attached to everything we do. Sometimes the risk is minute, sometimes massive; whatever the magnitude of the risk you take, by not transforming to the new way of business, you may find that you are:

■   Unhappy within yourself.

■   Becoming depressed.

■   Tolerating mediocrity.

■   Never achieving your full potential as a unique person.

- Always comparing yourself to others.

- Responding to fads and fashion whims within the field of HR.

- Feeling inadequate.

- Feeling increasingly dissatisfied.

- Suffering from time starvation.

- Rushing your life away,

- Asking questions like:

  - Why did I agree to ...

  - How do "they" think I must do this?

  - When will I ever get some "me" time?

  - Saying "yes" when you want to say "no!"

Don't hold back on making your ERP experience one that people will cherish and talk about for a long, long time.

1. Employee Lifecycle	2. Retirement Planning	3. Be Kind Practical, and Real	4. Begin Early Enough	5. Support is Vital	6. Prepare for the New Role	7. Welcome them to their New Role	8. The Final Goodbyes

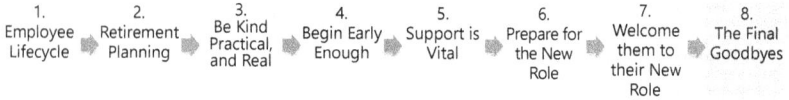

Summary of Chapter 7: Welcome Them to their New Role

1. Make the retiring employee feel as welcome as possible in the new role.

2. Be sure to communicate the impending change of role timeously and accurately.

3. Write a friendly communiqué to colleagues when informing them about the person's new role.

4. Remember to offer emotional support to the retiring employee during the time of change.

5. Do not refer to anybody's retirement in a transactional manner; be considerate.

Chapter 8

The Final Goodbyes...

Not all goodbyes are sad!

> Sometimes good-bye is a second chance. Clears your head.
> Anyway... missing someone makes you remember why you loved that person
> in the first place.
> Jamie McGuire, *Something Beautiful*

> **DID YOU KNOW?**
> *New employees who have not experienced a sound onboarding
> programme usually resign within 6-9 months. (Editor's research
> n= 350, 2012-2016)*

Introduction

It's so hard to leave something behind that made you happy. It's so
hard to close a chapter. It can be so painful to know you have to say
goodbye forever. It can hurt so much to part from something you
want but know you shouldn't keep. This opening paragraph taken
from *Exploring Your Mind*[30] is a most befitting introduction to our
final chapter, "The Final Goodbyes". Sometimes you just have to
turn the page and end a chapter. I know that all too well. You have
to change your job, lose a friend, the house is too small for so many
people. It's hard, sometimes really hard, but it's part of life. We close
one thing, say goodbye, and then open up another and say hello to
all the new things. The section below, is intended for both the HR
manager, project leader or any person who is championing the ERP,
as well as the employee.

You can add chapters to your life, but you need blank pages to keep on writing. That same old chapter needs an ending, it needs to be closed, but it will still be there. Traces of it will continue into the next page. It will all make sense once you know why you're closing it. It will all make sense when you let it. And part of this sense making, I believe, is that one establishes the new goal as soon as possible.

It's not easy to say goodbye. But it is good to know that once you've overcome the pain, you'll be ready for what's to come. Sometimes the pain of losing something is healthier than the pain of going on with that extra burden on your shoulders. That extra burden can be felt in the form of stress, illness or a host of other ills which befall us as we go about this tough thing called Life.

The emptiness after you say goodbye

It's not easy to explain, but everyone probably understands because we've all experienced it in one way or another. There are goodbyes that leave behind an emptiness that will be so hard to fill. Maybe you'll never fill it again. It's so hard to face the unknown, leave your comfort zone, and end something because it's so hard to realise you have to start another. It's true there's an emptiness, because the pain of loss is real pain, and covering it will only make it stronger later on. You have to learn to say goodbye, to handle that emptiness, and know when you have to close something. It might hurt right now, but it will stop hurting tomorrow.

You usually won't see the magic of saying goodbye right then. You'll see it in everything that comes afterwards. Believe me, a whole world of possibilities will open up to you. So much is waiting for you once you clean your wounds. The magic of saying goodbye is that it usually means saying hello to something else.

At this point it is important that, as an HR person, you have all your ducks in a row, that your ERP project is up to date and that you have the transition (farewell) party time, date and venue confirmed. Life must carry on, in the best possible way. If you learn to deal with that emptiness, if you don't make it bigger than it needs to be, if you give it the space it needs... If you let yourself cry when you need to, and give yourself time to heal, then you'll be ready for what comes. It's so hard to say goodbye, but once you do you'll heal and learn to take care of yourself. Learning to say goodbye is learning to grow.

A little girl will say goodbye to her red heart balloon.
You have to say goodbye to move forward.
You have to say goodbye to keep on moving; you have to end a chapter to start a new one. It may be time to throw yourself into something new. The world doesn't usually stop, and you're part of the world.

Fear, your faithful companion on the journey of life, will make you cling to what you know because you're afraid of what you don't know. But you have the strength to beat fear. If you look back you'll see how much your life changes. Not even you, with all the knowledge you have now, could have predicted exactly where you'd be right now. You've gotten to where you are now because of your decisions. And among your decisions was your decision to say goodbye.

It's time to learn how. It's hard to imagine the new things, the hello that comes after a goodbye. It's not easy, but it will definitely mean something good. It's so hard to say goodbye, but remember the magic in the new.

A couple of years ago, a middle-aged employee, Geoffrey, came to see me about a personal matter and to get some clarity on a few things. After some most interesting small talk, Geoffrey told me he was battling the demon of regret and it was consuming his life, impacting negatively on his family relationships and causing a few minor health concerns. When we got down to the details, his regret stemmed from not providing adequately for his financial security during retirement. At this time, he had 12 years (or 144 "paydays") left until age 65. Although the fact was absolutely true and he had a serious situation to contend with, he also had 12 years to do something about it. After some brainstorming and throwing some ideas around, Geoffrey left with a smile on his face and renewed hope – he now had a realistic plan! What's more, he was able to confide in another person who could listen, clarify understanding, ask a few questions and above all, just be there.

Please never, ever neglect, dear HR person, that part of your calling, job, responsibility – call it what you will – is to "be there". You must be the ray of hope, the constant factor, the stabiliser and the guardian of employees when they need you. If you do not have that in your nature somewhere, you will find it very difficult to remain in your role as honest-to-goodness, authentic HR specialist. Think about it!

Facing such a dramatic change as retiring is a truly transformative experience and one which one cannot easily forget; it becomes part of who you are. This brings to mind a great lesson I read about a couple years ago and I gladly share it with you.

Mexican Fisherman Meets Harvard MBA – What Really Matters in Life[31]

A vacationing American businessman standing on the pier of a quaint coastal fishing village in southern Mexico watched as a small boat with just one young Mexican fisherman pulled into the dock. Inside the small boat were several large yellowfin tuna. Enjoying the warmth of the early afternoon sun, the American complimented the Mexican on the quality of his fish.

> *"How long did it take you to catch them?" the American casually asked.*

> *"Oh, a few hours," the Mexican fisherman replied.*

> *"Why don't you stay out longer and catch more fish?" the American businessman then asked.*

The Mexican warmly replied, "With this I have more than enough to meet my family's needs."

The businessman then became serious, "But what do you do with the rest of your time?"

Responding with a smile, the Mexican fisherman answered, "I sleep late, play with my children, watch ball games, and take siesta with my wife. Sometimes in the evenings I take a stroll into the village to see my friends, play the guitar, and sing a few songs..."

The American businessman impatiently interrupted, "Look, I have an MBA from Harvard, and I can help you to be more profitable. You can start by fishing several hours longer every day. You can then sell the extra fish you catch. With the extra money, you can buy a bigger boat. With the additional income that larger boat will bring, before long you can buy a second boat, then a third one, and so on, until you have an entire fleet of fishing boats."

Proud of his own sharp thinking, he excitedly elaborated a grand scheme which could bring even bigger profits. "Then, instead of selling your catch to a middleman you'll be able to sell your fish directly to the processor, or even open your own cannery. Eventually, you could control the product, processing and distribution. You could leave this tiny coastal village and move to Mexico City, or possibly even Los Angeles or New York City, where you could even further expand your enterprise."

Having never thought of such things, the Mexican fisherman asked, "But how long will all this take?"

After a rapid mental calculation, the Harvard MBA pronounced, "Probably about 15-20 years, maybe less if you work really hard."

"And then what, señor?" asked the fisherman.

"Why, that's the best part!" answered the businessman with a laugh. "When the time is right, you would sell your company stock to the public and become very rich. You would make millions."

"Millions? Really? What would I do with it all?" asked the young fisherman in disbelief.

The businessman boasted, "Then you could happily retire with all the money you've made. You could move to a quaint coastal fishing village where you could sleep late, play with your grandchildren, watch ball games, and take siesta with your wife. You could stroll to the village in the evenings where you could play the guitar and sing with your friends all you want."

The moral of the story is: *Know what really matters in life, and you may find that it is already much closer than you think.*

You will be forgiven for thinking that the slant of this book is rather philosophical, sort of touch-feely, you know, the sort of things our hard-core colleagues sometimes accuse us of! Well, be reminded with honour and grace, that that is why we do what we do – people are our business and if we approach our business in a professional manner and with the elegance it deserves, the effect of the results on the bottom line will speak for themselves.

Back to the farewells and hellos of our retiring employee...

As the years and months roll by, we should also not forget that our retiree leaves a vacancy when they take on the new role. This means there is some work to be done to ensure that there is a smooth handover. Handover? Yes, handover! In the past, I have occasionally been in conflicting situations when the handover, and subsequent orientation, from the outgoing employee to the newcomer is less important that getting the newcomer "up and running" to meet the immediate needs. The results speak for themselves when either the new employee is disillusioned, regrets the decision to move to the new company and starts searching for other (better) opportunities almost immediately; or, the person tries to make it work (at all costs) and ends up suffering from burnout and then either leaving later on, or just warms their seat.

In Chapter 3, the retirement policy example provides a very clear and unambiguous guide as to how this transition should be handled; the following extract is particularly relevant:

__Role Transition__. As part of [organisation name] succession planning programme, role transition plans will be developed for [list positions and/or employee groups] to facilitate the transition process and transfer of knowledge. Human Resources and managers will develop individual transition plans for each retiring employee included in the succession planning programme.

The plans will include:

- *Accountabilities and expectations for the departing employee, their successor, and manager.*
- *Knowledge transfer requirements, methods, and timeline.*
- *The retiring employee's alternative work arrangements, if applicable.*

The following are the most commonly used knowledge transfer methods:

- *Mentoring.*
- *Job shadowing.*
- *Special assignments.*
- *[Insert method] All enquiries about the development of an appropriate transition plan should be directed to Human Resources [or insert specific position if available]. Note that if an employee has retired and is hired-back on a full or part time, contract or contingent basis the employee (will or will not) be eligible for additional benefits offered to employees.*

Quick Tip

Be sure to include the physical task transition from the retiring employee to the successor in your project plan. It will make your life a lot easier!

Let's do a quick "dipstick" test so make sure we are still on track in this chapter...

So far, the successor to the retiree has been discussed, how to make the best of the farewell is covered and we have checked that we are mindful of the company policy. Only two more things remain to be done before we get to the end and they are: 1) organising the farewell party, and 2) considering the possibility of alumni initiatives.

The farewell party or event need not be elaborate; however it must do justice to the transition of a valued employee. Amongst the influencing factors will be specific company preferences, budget, list of invitees and designated speakers. Whichever option is decided upon, be sure to cover the following aspects to ensure that people realise and understand that this is no ordinary event, it is significant and part of company strategy to attract, retain and respect the highest talent available.

1. Discuss the event's happenings with the retiree and successor so that they know what can be expected.

2. Decide on venue, menu and speakers right up front.

3. Communicate the reason and importance of the event very clearly.

4. Allow opportunity for co-worker stories, anecdotes and value-adds.

5. Do not forget to invite the successor to the event.

6. Be sure to include the "Welcome to the New Role" part of the event as well.

7. Make the connection between people, fun and organisational strategy.

And finally, on the matter of alumni initiatives:

According to Google Dictionary, an alumnus (plural noun: alumni) is a former pupil or student, of a particular school, college, or university or a former member of a group, company, or organisation. In short an alumni programme is a programme or project whereby former employees can contribute time and effort and assist in supporting the local community. In South Africa, the Broad-Based Black Economic Empowerment Act provides clear guidelines to legislative requirements in this regard. In short, be sure to create opportunities for former and current employees to reach out and make a positive difference.

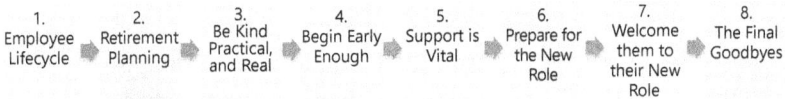

1. Employee Lifecycle	2. Retirement Planning	3. Be Kind Practical, and Real	4. Begin Early Enough	5. Support is Vital	6. Prepare for the New Role	7. Welcome them to their New Role	8. The Final Goodbyes

Summary of Chapter 8: The Final Goodbyes

1. Be prepared for the goodbyes and equip the retiree to do the same

2. Include the retiree's successor in this final stage more than ever before.

3. Plan and celebrate at an event that meets organisational requirements.

4. Remember to welcome the retiree to their new job.

5. Contemplate any alumni activities whereby employees can give back to the local community.

Conclusion

Now that you have come to the end of this book and have the opportunity to either feel very good about your organisation's ERP, are now better equipped to identify any gaps in your current ERP or whether you plan to start with a clean sheet, one thing is guaranteed... you will never see retirees in the same light as before reading this book.

Some of the facts, quick tips and quotes by some famous and some not-so-famous people, should give you food for thought. The following questions, to people in HR management or leadership positions, will hopefully stimulate more critical thinking and spark some other new ways of accommodating retiring employees and thereby giving hope to the individual concerned whilst simultaneously ensuring that your organisation is not squandering its assets for reasons of apathy or ignorance.

1. How can you ensure that you attract the best talent available?
2. Have any of your best employees left your employment and gone to another company for a lower salary? Why did this happen?
3. How would you define your company culture? Could an auditor ask any employee to describe the company culture and get a proper answer?
4. When last have you personally spoken to employees who will reach retirement age during the next 12 months?
5. Have you carefully thought about the options which could be available to retiring employees, should they opt to stay on for a second career?

Wishing you much prosperity, hope and success with the words of Desmond Tutu:

Your ordinary acts of love and hope
point to the extraordinary promise
that every human life is of inestimable value.

Endnotes

1   Morgan, J. (2017). *The Employee Experience Advantage: How to win the war for talent by giving employees the workspaces they want, the tools they need, and a culture they can celebrate.* Chapter 17: The Employee Life Cycle. Retrieved from: https://www.google.com/h?biw=1280&bi-h=721&tbm=isch&sa=1&ei=WaqkXKXgKvGCjLsP8K2KgA0&q=employ-ee+lifecycle+model&oq=employee+lifecycle&gs_l=img.1.3.35i39j0l9.44505.47380..49334...1.0..0.118.508.5j1......1....1..gws-wiz-img.gaLgwHX-AQ#imgdii=VmUq2FNTjHyikM:&imgrc=gPT2Pd8eCSmh_M:

2   Tuggle, K. (2015). *5 Hardest Things About Retirement That You Aren't Expecting.* Retrieved from: https://www.thestreet.com/sto-ry/13101438/1/5-hardest-things-about-retirement-that-you-arent-ex-pecting.html

3   Bieber, C. (2017). *5 Benefits of delaying retirement.* Retrieved from: https://money.cnn.com/2017/04/27/retirement/delay-retirement/index.html

4   Stats SA. (2019). *Quarterly Labour Force Survey, Quarter 2.* Retrieved from: http://www.statssa.gov.za/publications/P0211/P02112ndQuarter2019.pdf

5   Turner, A. (n.d.). *Retiring employees: 8 tips for a smooth transition.* Retrieved from: https://www.insperity.com/blog/retiring-employ-ees-8-tips-smooth-transition/

6   Ungashick. P, (2017) *Succession Planning Worksheet.* Retrieved from: https://www.vistage.com/wp-content/uploads/2017/02/Succession-PLanning-Chart.pdf

7   Stats SA. (2019). *Quarterly Labour Force Survey, Quarter 2.* Retrieved from: http://www.statssa.gov.za/publications/P0211/P02112ndQuarter2019.pdf

8   Hrala, J. (2019). *What is Phased Retirement?* Retrieved from: https://blog.careerminds.com/phased-retirement

9   HR Insider. (2015). *Retirement Policy.* Retrieved from: http://hrinsider.ca/wp-content/uploads/2015/03/Retirement-Policy.pdf

10 Lexico Dictionary. (n.d.). Definition of selection in English. Retrieved from: https://www.lexico.com/en/definition/selection

11 Google. (n.d.). Definition of 'Eligibility'. Retrieved from: https://www.google.com/search?q=eligibility&rlz=1C1CHZL_808&oq=eligibili-ty&aqs=chrome..69i57j69i59.134j0j8&sourceid=chrome&ie=UTF-8

12 Burke, R. (2008). *Project Management Techniques*. College edition. Auckland, New Zealand: Burke Publishing.

13 Hymowitz, C. (2016). *American Firms want to Keep Older Workers a Bit Longer*. Retrieved from: https://www.bloomberg.com/news/articles/2016-12-16/american-firms-want-to-keep-older-workers-a-bit-longer

14 Abella, A. (2018). *How to Allow Enough Time on Your Calendar for Projects*. Retrieved from: https://www.calendar.com/blog/how-to-allow-enough-time-on-your-calendar-for-projects/

15 Brans, P. (2011). *A Powerful Lesson in Time Management*. Quoted *Carol Dweck: How's Your Attitude?* Retrieved from: http://www.informit.com/articles/article.aspx?p=1688700

16 Refirement Network. (2016). *Quick SA Retirement Facts*. Retrieved from: https://www.refirementnetwork.com/2016/01/11/quick-sa-retirement-facts/

17 Rafter, D. (2014). *What Retirees Commonly Miss About Work*. Quoting Tom Hegna. Retrieved from: https://www.foxbusiness.com/features/what-retirees-commonly-miss-about-work

18 Laura, R. (2018). *Will you need a support group in retirement?* Retrieved from: https://www.forbes.com/sites/robertlaura/2018/02/28/will-you-need-a-support-group-in-retirement/#f99655a72d0b

19 Collins, J. (2001). *Good To Great*. New York, NY. HarperCollins Inc.

20 Thompson, N. (2018). *Transformation in 28 Days: To Achieving Your Best Health Ever*. Bloomington, IN: iUniverse

21 Kotter, J. (2018). *Video: Kotter's 8 steps leading change*. Retrieved from: https://www.youtube.com/watch?v=1QWiMkXyTP4

22 Kübler-Ross, E., & Kessler, D. (2005). *On grief and grieving: Finding the meaning of grief through the five stages of loss*. New York: Toronto: Scribner.

23 Ibid.

24 Glassdoor. (2017). *50 HR and Recruiting Stats for 2017*. Retrieved from: https://resources.glassdoor.com/rs/899-LOT-464/images/50hr-recruiting-and-statistics-2017.pdf

25 Venkatesh. (n.d.). *7 Principles of Communication – Explained!*. Retrieved from: http://www.yourarticlelibrary.com/management/communication/7-principles-of-communication-explained/53333

26 Veenman, D. & Cannon, D. (2014). The Strategic Importance of Conversations. *IEDP Developing Leaders*, Issue 15, pp 28-34.

27   Brackett, M., Rivers, S. & Salovey, P. (2011). Emotional Intelligence: Implications for Personal, Social, Academic, and Workplace Success. *Social and Personality Psychology Compass, 5,* 88-103. Yale University.

28   Goleman, D. (1996). *Emotional Intelligence.* New York: Bantam Books.

29   Schutte, N.S., Malouff, J.M., Thorsteinsson, E.B., Bhullar, N. & Rooke, S.E. (2007). A meta-analytic investigation of the relationship between emotional intelligence and health. *Personality and Individual Differences, 42,* 921-933.

30   Exploring your mind. (2018). *It's so hard to say goodbye.* Retrieved from: https://exploringyourmind.com/its-so-hard-to-say-goodbye/

31   WantToKnow.info. (n.d.). *What Really Matters in Life? Mexican Fisherman Meets Harvard MBA.* Retrieved from: https://www.wanttoknow.in-fo/051230whatmattersinlife

Index

www.ingramcontent.com/pod-product-compliance
Lightning Source LLC
Chambersburg PA
CBHW071528200326
41519CB00019B/6113